Journey

with God

FINDING PEACE *and* HAPPINESS

Gary Zimak

Published by The Word Among Us Press
7115 Guilford Drive, Suite 100
Frederick, Maryland 21704
wau.org

25 24 23 22 21   1 2 3 4 5

ISBN: 978-1-59325-554-1
eISBN: 978-1-59325-556-5

Design by Suzanne Earl

To Mom and Dad (Gerry and Ed Zimak)

I'm so grateful for all your love throughout the years. Never once did I feel unloved. Most important, thank you for starting me off on my journey with God when I was still an infant. I miss you so much, but I look forward to the day when we'll be together again. I love you!

Contents

PART THREE: SERVING GOD

Introduction

The desire for God is written in the human heart, because man is created by God and for God; and God never ceases to draw man to himself. Only in God will he find the truth and happiness he never stops searching for.

—*Catechism of the Catholic Church, 27*

I definitely know what it's like to search for happiness. In fact, I spent decades pursuing it in every way I reasonably could. Every way but God, that is.

Sure, I went to Catholic school for twelve years, tossed up a prayer every once in a while, and never missed Sunday Mass, but I can't honestly say that I ever thought of God as a legitimate source of happiness. TV, music, junk food, beer, hanging out with friends—absolutely. But God? No way. He just wasn't real enough.

Like many others, I began to settle; I concluded that life wasn't meant to be fun. My unofficial goal was to dull the pain and drudgery of daily life and make it to the weekend. Even though none of my go-to sources of happiness were delivering for me, I kept pursuing them. After all, a little pleasure here and there is better than nothing. Somehow I made it through panic attacks, loneliness, and feelings of inadequacy. In my mind, I was doing as well as one could do in a world filled with trials and suffering.

Every now and then, however, I thought about God as a possible source of happiness. Maybe he really could help me. Maybe there was something to this religion thing. On a few occasions, I gave it a shot. I'd pray, read the Bible, even go to prayer meetings. I'd feel better for a while, but it was too much work. Before long, I'd be back to seeking pleasure in the "normal" ways.

Finally, a health crisis in 2004 led me to step up my effort to seek God. To make a long story short, I began to experience unusual symptoms (not good for someone with a history of hypochondria!) and assumed that I was dying. Now, with my back against the wall, I finally made the decision to turn to God and truly give him a chance. After years of living a life filled with anxiety and misery, the time for fooling around was over. Now I was serious!

Journeying with God

> Behold, I stand at the door and knock; if any one hears my voice and opens the door, I will come in to him and eat with him, and he with me.
>
> —Revelation 3:20

I didn't realize it at the time, but I was actually on a journey with God. The *Catechism* states that God "never ceases to call every man to seek him, so as to find life and happiness" (30), and I can vouch for the accuracy of that statement. I now understand that those "maybe I should consider God" thoughts were coming from him. He kept reaching out to me, trying to give me the happiness I sought, but I was too busy trying to find it in other ways.

Before we begin to explore what it means to journey with God, it's probably a good idea to step back and define faith. We use the word so often that sometimes we take its meaning for granted. In a general sense, faith is placing our trust in someone or something. In this book, however, we'll be looking at Christian faith or the virtue of faith. And while it does involve trust, it also has a deeper meaning.

According to the Bible, faith is "the assurance of things hoped for, the conviction of things not seen" (Hebrews 11:1). The *Catechism* defines it as "man's response to God, who reveals himself and gives himself to man, at the same time bringing man a superabundant light as he searches for the ultimate meaning of his life" (26).

Putting it all together, faith is God's revelation to us and our response to that revelation. It's not the same as walking in darkness, although it does involve some degree of uncertainty and trust. Essentially, stepping out in faith involves trusting that God is who he says he is and that he will keep his promises. It can be a little scary at first, but it gets easier over time. The more we place our trust in God, the more we realize just how trustworthy he is.

For many of us, faith was (or is) an intellectual exercise. In other words, here are the facts about God, and here is a list of how we should behave. Does that sound familiar?

If so, it's no wonder that life can be so frightening and empty at times. No wonder God seems so distant. No wonder it's so difficult to share the good news with others. Something is obviously missing.

Faith Is a Relationship

Learning the facts is only part of the journey of faith—and a relatively small part, in all honesty. More than anything else, the journey of faith is about a relationship. It's about getting to know almighty God, the Creator of the universe.

Yes, it involves learning the facts about him and the teachings of his Church. But above all, it is about spending time in his presence and growing in an intimate relationship with the Father, Son, and Holy Spirit. It's about living in the presence of Jesus, who came to teach us about the Father, save us from our sins, and anoint us with his Spirit. Through Jesus, we gain the privilege of becoming adopted sons and daughters of God. No longer is God a distant or impersonal figure but our "Abba" Father. Suddenly our journey of faith becomes extremely personal.

As I look back on my own journey with God (which is very much ongoing), I can see that it has come down to the three steps familiar to many of us from childhood religion classes: *knowing God, loving God,* and *serving God.* These three steps, typically practiced simultaneously, comprise the journey of faith for all of us.

As you progress through this book, you'll learn simple and effective methods for knowing, loving, and serving God. You'll learn to spend time in his presence and encounter him in the duties of daily life. Best of all, you'll discover an important lesson that many people never grasp: that the journey with God is also the journey of happiness. Every step made toward God is a step toward greater happiness.

I invite you to join me on the journey. Together we'll discover how Jesus, the Father, the Holy Spirit, Mary, Joseph, and the angels and saints are present on the journey. We'll look at common pitfalls and ways to avoid them. We'll also tackle the hard questions and learn how to respond when God's actions don't seem to make sense.

No matter where you are on your journey with God—beginner, intermediate, advanced—you can benefit from this book. I can say that with confidence because I conclude each chapter with a prayer to a Person of the Trinity. The Father, Son, and Holy Spirit know exactly who you are and what you need. They will provide the additional one-on-one tutoring that will get you where you need to be.

As the old Chinese proverb states, "A journey of a thousand miles begins with a single step." The same holds true for the journey with God. It begins with one step, and it continues step-by-step. Try not to dwell on where you are or how far you need to go. Instead focus on beginning—or continuing—the journey by taking a single step. If you're ready, let's take that next step together.

. . . .

Heavenly Father, thank you for creating me and desiring that I enter into an intimate relationship with you. Please awaken your Holy Spirit in me, so that I may better understand and feel your love for me. Help me also to be aware of your constant presence and your ability to handle any problem that I will ever face. Above all, I ask that you allow me to grow closer to you as I progress through this book.

I ask this in the name of Jesus, your Son. Amen.

Draw near to God and he will draw near to you. (James 4:8)

PART ONE

KNOWING GOD

Man's faculties make him capable of coming to a knowledge of the existence of a personal God. But for man to be able to enter into real intimacy with him, God willed both to reveal himself to man and to give him the grace of being able to welcome this revelation in faith. The proofs of God's existence, however, can predispose one to faith and help one to see that faith is not opposed to reason.

—Catechism, 35

God wants me to know him! That's definitely good news, but it can be a little overwhelming.

What exactly does it mean to know him? Is it a matter of poring over the Bible and other spiritual books, trying to learn as much about him as possible? Or is there something more?

Simply put, the answer is yes to both options. Knowing God involves learning as much as possible about him, but it also involves spending time with him. Doing one without the other will hinder our efforts to know God intimately, as he desires.

In order to know God and enter into a deep relationship with him, it will help if you understand three key facts: God loves you; God is with you; God is bigger than your problems.

You might be tempted to say, "Who doesn't know that?" Please don't make that mistake. Failing to truly understand these concepts is the cause of needless anxiety, hopelessness, and discouragement.

We'll spend an entire chapter on each of these points, but for now, take a minute, and reflect on how your life could look if you believed with all your heart that God loves you, is with you, and can easily handle any problem you will ever face. With that in mind, let's get ready to enter the first phase of our journey with God.

CHAPTER 1

God Loves You

For this reason I bow my knees before the Father, from whom every family in heaven and on earth is named, that according to the riches of his glory he may grant you to be strengthened with might through his Spirit in the inner man, and that Christ may dwell in your hearts through faith; that you, being rooted and grounded in love, may have power to comprehend with all the saints what is the breadth and length and height and depth, and to know the love of Christ which surpasses knowledge, that you may be filled with all the fulness of God.

—Ephesians 3:14-19

God loves you. Of course he does. Who doesn't know that, right? But even though we may have heard that message countless times, we could all use a better understanding of what God's love for us actually means.

Frankly, this message meant nothing to me for many years. It fell into the same category as the sky is blue and the ocean is deep. God's love for me was such a vague concept that it didn't make any difference in my daily life.

What I ultimately discovered, however, is that we can never be at peace unless we begin to understand the depth of God's love for us. Life can be difficult. We all encounter challenges, some of which can rob us of hope. It's easy to feel peaceful when everything is going our way, but that feeling can disappear in an instant. Without a thorough understanding of God's love for us, our peace will vanish as soon as we encounter the next problem.

The goal of this chapter is to help you realize, not just that God loves you, but *how much* he loves you. And I want you to feel his love in your heart, not merely know about it with your intellect. As you come to a greater understanding of his love for you as a unique, precious individual, life will no longer seem like a series of random events. Instead, you will be able to see the loving hand of your heavenly Father working in your life.

What Is Love?

Before we can appreciate how much God loves us, we must understand exactly what love is. The word is so familiar, and we use it so frequently, that typically we don't give much thought to its meaning. We take it for granted that we know what it means to love something or someone. But do we really?

Most dictionary definitions of love mention feelings or emotion. It's true that feelings of affection often accompany love, but they're not necessary. Jesus commands us to "love one another" (John 13:34). He expects us to take action, to make a conscious decision to love even if the feelings aren't there. We may not be able to control our feelings, but we can choose to love someone.

What exactly does it mean to love someone? According to St. Thomas Aquinas, "To love is to will the good of another" (*Catechism*, 1766). When we act in a way that puts the needs of others before our own needs, we are truly loving. The ultimate form of that love is known as *unconditional* love, which means that there are no conditions or strings attached. When I love someone in this way, nothing they say or do can affect my love for them. Loving someone unconditionally means loving them for who they are, not for how they behave.

Expressing Love

We express love for others through our actions. Any act of kindness done for another person is an example of love in action. These acts include praying, offering a kind word or deed, giving a gift, letting someone have the last word, avoiding gossip, and offering anything else that can benefit another person in any way. Good feelings may or may not accompany these actions, but the lack of good feelings in no way negates the action of loving. In fact, when good feelings are absent and we love anyway, we are truly sacrificing for the good of another.

In a similar way, but to a greater degree, God loves each of us. According to St. John, not only does God love us, but God *is* love (see 1 John 4:16). He loves us totally and unconditionally. There is nothing you and I can ever do to make him love us any more or any less. His love for every human being who ever lived or ever will live is 100-percent perfect. This means that he loves every child abuser, mass murderer, and terror-ist every bit as much as he loved Mother Teresa and Pope St. John Paul II.

Let that sink in for a minute. It's a difficult concept to pro-cess, but we must understand it in order to appreciate the enormity of God's love.

To make it more personal, think of the greatest offense you ever committed, and then think of the kindest act you ever performed. As hard as it may be to imagine, God loved you exactly the same amount at both of those moments. No matter what we do or don't do, nothing can affect how much God loves us.

The parable of the prodigal son illustrates the power of the Father's love for us (see Luke 15:11-32). The parable cen-ters on a man who had two sons, one of whom demanded his inheritance and then squandered it on loose living and self-in-dulgence. When he had spent all he had, the desperate son was forced to work in the fields, feeding pigs. Realizing that his father's servants had better food to eat than he did, the prodi-gal son decided to return home and beg his father to take him back as a servant.

> And he arose and came to his father. But while he was
> yet at a distance, his father saw him and had compas-
> sion, and ran and embraced him and kissed him. And the
> son said to him, "Father, I have sinned against heaven
> and before you; I am no longer worthy to be called your
> son." But the father said to his servants, "Bring quickly
> the best robe, and put it on him; and put a ring on his
> hand, and shoes on his feet; and bring the fatted calf

> and kill it, and let us eat and make merry; for this my son
> was dead, and is alive again; he was lost, and is found."
> And they began to make merry. (Luke 15:20-24)

The love of the father for his repentant son is obvious. Two easily overlooked details, however, take that love to the next level.

First, the father, full of compassion, ran, embraced, and kissed his son *before* the son even asked for forgiveness. The father's love didn't depend on his son asking to be forgiven. He loved him unconditionally.

Second, the fact that the father *ran* illustrates just how anxious he was to welcome his son. He couldn't wait. That's an example of how God loves each of us, even when we separate ourselves from him by sin.

God Knows You

It's possible to love someone without knowing them, but it's impossible to enter into a deep relationship with someone unless you do know them. The focus of the first part of this book is on knowing God, but it's also important to appreciate just how well God knows you. It may surprise you to discover that he knows you better than you know yourself. In no way is he a distant being in a faraway place, uninvolved in your life. He is close to you at every moment; he never lets you out of his sight.

We see a great example of this in the life of Sarah's maid, Hagar (see Genesis 16). After Sarah rejected her, Hagar ran away, and she ended up having an encounter with the Lord. Overwhelmed to discover that God was looking out for her, she gave him the name *El Roi*, or "the God who sees." The Revised New Jerusalem Bible preserves the original Hebrew in its translation:

> Hagar gave a name to the LORD who had spoken to her, "You are El Roi," saying, "Have I really seen him who looks after me?" (Genesis 16:13, RNJB)

Have you ever thought someone didn't know you existed, only to discover that they did? It's a great feeling.

I remember prepping my parents for back-to-school night when I was a sophomore in high school. As I went over the list of teachers, I told them that my history teacher didn't know who I was. In my younger days, I was extremely shy, and I was used to being ignored.

Unaware that my parents had mentioned this to the teacher, I was astonished when he came up to me in class the following day and said, with a smile, "Mr. Zimak, I *do* know who you are!" At first I felt a little foolish, but then I began to feel special. I wasn't an unknown student after all!

Need more evidence that God knows you intimately? If you have any doubts, start by reading Psalm 139. It will change your thinking. Not only does God know you personally, but he is aware of your thoughts and even knows when you sit or stand.

> O LORD, you have searched me and known me!
> You know when I sit down and when I rise up;
> you discern my thoughts from afar. (Psalm 139:1-2)

The psalm goes on to state that God created us in our mother's womb:

> For you formed my inward parts,
>   you knitted me together in my mother's womb. (Psalm 139:13)

It gets even better. Not only does God know us, but he knew all about us before we even existed.

> Your eyes beheld my unformed substance;
>   in your book were written, every one of them,
> the days that were formed for me,
>   when as yet there was none of them. (Psalm 139:16)

God created you according to detailed specifications, and you are wonderfully made. He knows you from the inside out and is with you at all times. His love is unsurpassed by any earthly love. You are very precious to him.

How Do I Know God Loves Me?

The best and most basic place to begin in knowing God loves you is with the fact that he created you. Even though he is all-powerful and lacks nothing, God created you so that you could share in his happiness both now and in heaven. This is a great example of God's love that we rarely consider. Caught up in the details of life, we fail to recognize that our existence is not accidental.

God consciously chose to create us, not because we could add anything to his happiness, but so that we could experience the joy of life in him. He did this for no other reason but that he loves us.

We can also gain insight from the pages of the Bible. One of the most popular verses in all of Scripture states that the incarnation of Jesus was an expression of God's love for us: "For God so loved the world that he gave his only-begotten Son, that whoever believes in him should not perish but have eternal life" (John 3:16).

When we look at the life of Jesus and examine all that he said and did, we see love in action. Even though we don't deserve it, Jesus willingly endured an agonizing death so that we could be reconciled with the Father. He didn't belong on the cross; we did. He took our place as an act of love.

If we pause to think about it, we can begin to appreciate the love found in the sacrifice of Jesus. This sometimes fails to register because we're bombarded with the problems of life. But I have a few tricks up my sleeve that can help you enter more fully into God's love. Consider the following.

Did you ever stop and think about all the things you've enjoyed over the course of your life? Off the top of my head, I can recall the pleasure of warm summer days, playing with my childhood friends, reading comic books, listening to the radio, eating great meals at restaurants, spending time with my wife and children, going on vacation, encountering Jesus in prayer, watching baseball, and on and on. I may not have thought about it at the time, but all this enjoyment is a gift from God. Because he loves me, he has devised countless ways that allow me to enjoy life.

If you spend five or ten minutes reviewing your life, I know you can come up with a comparable list of little gifts from God. That's love!

But what if you've reviewed all the concrete signs of God's love for you and still don't feel it? Don't panic. Sometimes examining the evidence isn't enough to convince us.

In his Letter to the Romans, St. Paul tells us that "God's love has been poured into our hearts through the Holy Spirit" (Romans 5:5). Try asking the Holy Spirit to fill your heart with God's love and allow you to really feel it. Get into the habit of doing this every day. In my experience, this doesn't always work instantly, but over time I begin to know *and feel* that God loves me. Give it a try, and see for yourself.

Obstacles

Several obstacles may block our ability to believe that God loves us. Let's take a closer look at a few of them and look for ways to overcome their impact. We'll start with the one that, in my opinion, affects more people than any other obstacle.

Why Does God Let Bad Things Happen?

This can be a deal breaker for many people. There's just no getting around the fact that bad things happen. Death and suffering are very much a part of life. And it seems that some people experience more than their share of suffering. If God is all-powerful and truly loves us, why does he allow bad things to happen?

Some suffering can be attributed to free will—people can choose to do bad things—but that doesn't explain why, for example, earthquakes and hurricanes often occur in impoverished areas. Aren't those people suffering enough? Why does God allow them to suffer even more?

No matter how hard we try, we will never be able to grasp why God allows evil to happen. Our human understanding is too limited. If we could always understand his thinking, then he wouldn't be God.

Although we don't know why God allows some bad things to happen, we do know that he can bring good out of them. Does it make sense that Jesus had to die on the cross to redeem us? Maybe not to us, but it made sense to God.

It's difficult to find a person who suffered more than Job. Even though he was "blameless and upright, one who feared God, and turned away from evil" (Job 1:1), the Lord permitted Satan to tempt Job with a variety of trials and tribulations. Throughout the Book of Job, the suffering man and his friends had plenty to say, but God remained silent. Finally, God decided to speak, and he asked Job some questions of his own:

> "Where were you when I laid the foundation of the earth?
>   Tell me, if you have understanding.
> Who determined its measurements—surely you know!"
> (Job 38:4-5)

That was only the beginning. For the next four chapters (see Job 38-41), God hammered Job with what seemed like an endless series of questions. In the midst of the barrage, Job had a chance to reply:

> "Behold, I am of small account; what shall I answer you?
>   I lay my hand on my mouth.
> I have spoken once, and I will not answer;
>   twice, but I will proceed no further." (Job 40:4-5)

Job acknowledged that he had no good answers to the Lord's questions, but the Lord subjected him to more of the same. Then Job had the chance to make one final statement:

> "I know that you can do all things,
>   and that no purpose of yours can be thwarted.
> 'Who is this that hides counsel without knowledge?'
> Therefore I have uttered what I did not understand,
>   things too wonderful for me, which I did not know.
> 'Hear, and I will speak;
>   I will question you, and you declare to me.'
> I had heard of you by the hearing of the ear,
>   but now my eye sees you;
> therefore I despise myself,
>   and repent in dust and ashes." (Job 42:2-6)

Humbling himself, Job repented and admitted that he was wrong for questioning God's actions. He learned a lesson that we all learn at some point: there are some things in life that won't make sense to us. That's totally normal.

Try not to let this overwhelm you. Just as children shouldn't be expected to understand all their parents' actions, we should not expect to understand everything that God does or allows.

I'm Not Worthy

This mindset is based on the false belief that we must do something to earn God's love. It stems from a failure to understand the concept of unconditional love. As we have already discussed, there is nothing we can do to make God love us any more or any less. He loves each of us, not because of what we do, but because of who we are.

Jesus entered our world to help us better understand the Father. To that end, we learn a powerful lesson about the Father's unconditional love on the day of Jesus' baptism. After Jesus came out of the water, a voice from heaven proclaimed, "This is my beloved Son, with whom I am well pleased" (Matthew 3:17).

Did the Father love Jesus because of something he did? Was he pleased with him because of his great works? Not at all. At this point, Jesus hadn't even started his public ministry. The Father loved him and was pleased with him because of who he was, not because of what he did. That's how the Father loves you too.

I Just Don't Feel It

One of the biggest mistakes human beings make is placing too much emphasis on feelings. The fact that we feel something doesn't make it true. You might not be able to feel God's love, but he still loves you.

The best way to deal with this obstacle is to face it head-on. No matter how close you are to the Lord, you will not always feel his love. That doesn't mean there's something wrong with you; it simply means that you're human, and your feelings don't always express reality.

When I can't feel God's love, I remind myself that he loves me, and I move on. Typically my heart will catch up with my head at some point.

Toward the beginning of the COVID-19 pandemic, my wife struggled with crippling anxiety. Eventually this led Eileen to rely more on God and grow closer to him, so in one sense, her anxiety was a blessing. But after several weeks of sleepless nights and stress-filled days (for both of us), the "blessing" was getting old, and we were ready to move on.

I remember getting angry with God one night and telling him that he wasn't helping matters. Eileen was begging for peace and not getting it. How was that helping her?

Needless to say, I wasn't feeling his love for either one of us, and I had to resort to my head knowledge. Despite his apparent lack of response, I still knew that God loved us. That knowledge was enough to get me through some very difficult days.

> For I am sure that neither death, nor life, nor angels, nor principalities, nor things present, nor things to come, nor powers, nor height, nor depth, nor anything else in all creation, will be able to separate us from the love of God in Christ Jesus our Lord. (Romans 8:38-39)

Looking Back, Looking Ahead

Before moving on to the next chapter, spend five or ten minutes with the Father in prayer. Ask the Holy Spirit to help you call to mind the many ways God expresses his love for you; pray for a greater understanding of the depths of his love. Thank your heavenly Father for creating you, for providing for all your needs, and for sending Jesus to redeem you. Don't forget to offer thanks for the trials and difficulties through which the Lord has brought you.

In the next chapter, we'll explore another fact about God: he is always with us. Just wait until you see the many ways he makes his presence known!

• •

Heavenly Father, I praise and worship you. I may not always feel it, but I know that you love me with an unconditional love. Please increase my awareness of your love and of your desire to provide for all my needs. May the Holy Spirit inspire all my thoughts, words, and deeds so that they give you glory. I ask this in Jesus' name. Amen.

CHAPTER 2

God Is with You

Be strong and of good courage; be not frightened, neither be dismayed; for the LORD your God is with you wherever you go.

—Joshua 1:9

Even though decades have passed, I vividly remember the first time I drove a car. I was sixteen years old, had completed several driver's education sessions, and had looked forward to this day for a long time. Nevertheless, I was terrified that something would go wrong. What if I panicked and got into an accident? What if I injured myself or someone else? An endless list of what-ifs filled my mind, and I was overcome with fear.

As I was worrying about what might happen, however, a couple of thoughts popped into my mind. They brought me comfort and took away some of my fear.

First, I realized that I wouldn't be alone in the car; my driving instructor would be with me. If I were confused or unsure about what to do, he'd help me.

Second, I recalled that the car was equipped with two steering wheels and two brake pedals. Not only would my instructor be able to advise me, but he would also have the power to take charge and keep me from getting into trouble.

Suddenly my fear began to fade. The more I thought about it, the better I felt. Now, instead of being afraid, I once again looked forward to driving a car for the first time.

God's Constant Presence

Just as the presence of my driving instructor allowed me to relax behind the wheel, the presence of God in my life makes it possible for me to live without fear. As a person who tends to be anxious, I can find the uncertainty of life extremely challenging. I like to know what lies ahead, and I want it to be good. If I know that no suffering will be heading my way tomorrow, then I'll be able to enjoy today.

Of course, life doesn't work that way. If I can be at peace only in the absence of conflict and under favorable circumstances, it's never going to happen. Is there an alternative?

Fortunately, God offers a totally realistic and effective approach to living peacefully. Unlike my preferred problem-free way, his way is completely achievable and based on reality: he offers to be present to me at all times. The Creator of the universe, who holds the world in his hands, is willing to walk with me as I navigate the challenges of daily life.

Choosing to accept his offer is a wise move. When I remember to do so, I find myself filled with peace. When I forget and try to eliminate all problems from my life, I'm filled with anxiety.

Unfortunately, it can be difficult to be aware of God's constant presence. We'll look at some of the specific obstacles later in this chapter, but for now I want you to understand that losing sight of God is a common problem. Life can be challenging, and it's easy to get caught up in our struggles. Nevertheless, focusing on God's constant presence is a surefire way to retain your peace, even in the midst of the storm.

Life Can Be Frightening

The Bible frequently encourages us to "be not afraid." It has been said that these words (or variations of them) appear in the Bible 365 times—one for each day. While that exact number is open to debate, depending on your version of the Bible, both the Old and New Testaments repeatedly tell us to put aside fear.

I can't speak for the Holy Spirit, but I can offer an educated guess as to why this message appears so often in Sacred Scripture. Probably because we are so afraid!

Why are so many of us filled with fear? That's easy to understand. Even though we work extremely hard to ensure that everything goes smoothly in our lives, there is only so much we can do. We have limited control over our circumstances. Based on my own battles with anxiety, I can confirm one thing: anxiety typically sets in when we try to control the uncontrollable.

What exactly is outside our control, you may wonder? Just about everything. The COVID-19 pandemic has made this clear, forcing many of us to confront our mortality and vulnerability.

If this is true—if we are not in control—why would God repeatedly tell us that we must not be afraid? After all, what could be more frightening than having no control in a world where bad things happen every day? It might help to stop and ask yourself, "What lies at the heart of my fear?"

For many of us, I think, the answer is that we attempt to handle problems on our own, without God's ever-present help. Yes, life is tough, but only when we try to handle it alone. God never intended for us to be self-sufficient, and that is precisely why he can tell us to have no fear. We sometimes focus so much on the "be not afraid" message that we miss the truth underlying this statement: there is one reason, and one reason alone, that we can set aside fear: God is with us.

You Are Never Alone

I think that it's great that "be not afraid" is such a strong theme in the Bible, along with the message that God is with us always and everywhere. Yet sometimes it's difficult for me to believe that almighty God, the Creator of the universe, cares enough about me to follow me around and get involved in my life.

When you think about it, though, this is really a natural extension of a fact that we've already established: God loves us. Throughout history, God has never abandoned his people. Even when they turned their backs on him, he was always watching over them and devising ways to guide them to safety.

Before we look at some of the ways the Lord is present to us, let's look at some of his words in the Bible. Over and over, he assures us that no matter where, no matter when, no matter what, "I am with you!"

"Be Strong"

As the Israelites were about to enter the Promised Land, they received some potentially unsettling news. God was going to replace their leader, Moses, with the much younger Joshua. The Lord decided that Joshua would be the person to lead them across the Jordan River into Canaan, a fact that could easily have shaken the confidence of the people.

In an attempt to comfort the Israelites, Moses spoke to them, pointing out something they needed to remember:

> "Be strong and of good courage, do not fear or be in dread . . . : for it is the Lord your God who goes with you; he will not fail you or forsake you." (Deuteronomy 31:6)

Fully aware that the success of their journey thus far didn't depend on him, Moses comforted his people by assuring them of God's continued presence. In no way did he promise them an adventure free of problems or struggles. Instead, he urged them to have no fear because God would be with them. He would not fail or forsake them.

God will be with you. What could be more comforting than hearing those words from a holy man like Moses? How about hearing those words directly from the mouth of God?

"Fear Not"

That's exactly what happened to the prophet Isaiah when the Lord gave him a message for the Israelites. Essentially, the message for Isaiah was the same as the one Moses delivered to the Israelites, but this time God himself spoke the words:

> Fear not, for I am with you,
>   be not dismayed, for I am your God;
> I will strengthen you, I will help you,
>   I will uphold you with my victorious right hand.
> (Isaiah 41:10)

As someone who has felt called to do something frightening—move from the software industry into full-time ministry—I appreciate the value of these words. The Lord hasn't spoken audibly to me, but I have heard him tell me, many times since that move, "Fear not."

"I Will Be with You"

Would you like another example of someone who needed God's reassurance? Let's look at the story of Gideon (see Judges 6).

After being freed from slavery in Egypt, the Israelites were poverty-stricken and suffering under the oppression of the Midianites. This went on for seven years. One day, while working in the fields, Gideon encountered an angel of the Lord, who delivered a familiar message: the Lord is with you. On hearing these words, Gideon raised a good question: if the Lord is with us, why are these bad things happening?

The Lord then communicated an unexpected message. He told Gideon to deliver his people from the oppression of the Midianites. The young man responded in an honest manner: "Please, Lord, how can I deliver Israel? Behold, my clan is the weakest in Manas'seh, and I am the least in my family" (Judges 6:15).

Sounds reasonable, doesn't it? Gideon's words are yet another version of the "you picked the wrong guy, Lord" message that appears throughout the Bible—whenever God asks someone to do something difficult. The Lord's answer? "But I will be with you, and you shall strike the Mid'ianites as one man" (Judges 6:16).

You will not fail, because "I will be with you" (Judges 6:16). Over and over again, we see that message repeated in the pages of the Old Testament.

Jesus delivered the same message as he prepared to ascend into heaven. In what is known as the Great Commission, Jesus sent the apostles out into the world to continue his mission of spreading the good news. He reminded them (and us) of something we should never forget:

> Go therefore and make disciples of all nations, baptizing them in the name of the Father and of the Son and of the Holy Spirit, teaching them to observe all that I have commanded you; and behold, I am with you always, to the close of the age. (Matthew 28:19-20)

This memorable message closes out Matthew's Gospel. The Lord is with us—not for a month, a year, a decade, or a thousand years, but until the end of time.

How Is God Present?

As we have established, God is accessible to us at all times and in all situations. We sometimes describe this attribute of God by stating that he is omnipresent, or present everywhere.

No discussion of God's presence would be complete, however, without touching on some of the specific ways in which he is present to us. And though it's true that he is present in everything, from nature to our fellow human beings, let's concentrate on what I consider the three most important manifestations of God's presence: Jesus, the Holy Spirit, and the word of God.

Jesus

A startling event some two thousand years ago pretty much dispels any argument that God is uninvolved and distant. In an instant, something happened that forever changed the course of history: "And the Word became flesh and dwelt among us, full of grace and truth; we have beheld his glory, glory as of the only-begotten Son from the Father" (John 1:14).

God loved the world so much that he sent his only Son to take on human flesh, live among us, suffer, die, and rise from the dead so that we could live in heaven forever (see John 3:16). No words adequately describe the enormity of that event. For the purpose of our discussion, however, I invite you to consider the fact that God loves you so much that he wants to literally enter into your world and live for and with you.

Citing the prophet Isaiah (see Isaiah 7:14) and noting the birth of Jesus, Matthew reminds us of something critically important about the name Emmanuel:

> Behold, a virgin shall conceive and bear a son,
> and his name shall be called Emmanuel" (which means,
> God with us). (Matthew 1:23)

In Jesus, fully present in the Eucharist and in all the sacraments, God is literally with us always, everywhere, and forever.

The Holy Spirit

Just before entering into his passion and death, Jesus promised his followers that he would not abandon them. That promise would be fulfilled in the third Person of the Trinity—the Holy Spirit.

> And I will ask the Father, and he will give you another Counselor, to be with you for ever, even the Spirit of truth, whom the world cannot receive, because it neither sees him nor knows him; you know him, for he dwells with you, and will be in you. (John 14:16-17)

We first receive the Holy Spirit in Baptism; in Confirmation we receive the "special outpouring of the Holy Spirit," bringing "an increase and deepening of baptismal grace" (*Catechism*, 1302, 1303). The Spirit is sometimes referred to as the forgotten

Person of the Trinity, and often we overlook or downplay his role. This is understandable because we can't see him at work, but the Holy Spirit plays a huge role in our spiritual life.

Not only does the Spirit make God present to us, but he makes him present inside us. Think about that for a minute. In the Holy Spirit, God is not just with you, but he is in you. He can't get much closer than that!

Because the Holy Spirit doesn't seek attention, however, you are free to overlook his role in your life. Don't let that happen. Give the Spirit permission to transform you into the image of Jesus and lead you into a closer relationship with your heavenly Father. It's as simple as praying, "Come, Holy Spirit." Those three words can be life changing when you pray them on a regular basis.

The Word (Scripture and Tradition)

Another way that God is present to us is through his word. As Catholics, we absolutely believe that God speaks to us through Sacred Scripture. In addition, we believe that he speaks through Sacred Tradition. According to the *Catechism*,

> "Sacred Tradition and Sacred Scripture, then, are bound closely together and communicate one with the other. For both of them, flowing out from the same divine well-spring, come together in some fashion to form one thing, and move towards the same goal." Each of them makes present and fruitful in the Church the mystery of Christ, who promised to remain with his own "always, to the close of the age."

"*Sacred Scripture* is the speech of God as it is put down in writing under the breath of the Holy Spirit."

"And [Holy] *Tradition* transmits in its entirety the Word of God which has been entrusted to the apostles by Christ the Lord and the Holy Spirit. It transmits it to the successors of the apostles so that, enlightened by the Spirit of truth, they may faithfully preserve, expound, and spread it abroad by their preaching."

As a result the Church, to whom the transmission and interpretation of Revelation is entrusted, "does not derive her certainty about all revealed truths from the holy Scriptures alone. Both Scripture and Tradition must be accepted and honored with equal sentiments of devotion and reverence." (*Catechism, 80–82*, quoting Vatican II, *Dei Verbum* 9; Matthew 28:20)

Not only is God present to us always and everywhere, but he continues to speak to us though his word. In order to hear him, however, we have to listen. The gifts of Sacred Scripture and Sacred Tradition greatly simplify that process, but ultimately, the choice to listen is up to us. It pretty much goes without saying, but I'll say it anyway: choosing to listen to God's voice is always a good idea.

Obstacles

You probably don't need me to tell you that it's easy to overlook God's presence. Unless we take some concrete steps to remind ourselves that we are never alone, we can forget the reality of God's omnipresence. Let's look at a few of the more common obstacles and explore ways to overcome them.

You Want Me to Believe What?

I tend to be cynical. When I take my car in for service and they promise to have it ready at a certain time, I don't always believe them. The same goes for campaign promises and people who tell me that a certain home project is no big deal.

Some of my skepticism is due to past experience, and some of it is due to my analytical nature. Also, for thirty years I worked as a software developer and was trained to view everything with a degree of skepticism. If I have a hard time believing that a political candidate will deliver on his promises or my car will be ready on time, imagine how difficult it must be for me to believe in the power of the sacraments or an invisible God's presence in my life.

God understands that he asks us to believe many hard-to-believe concepts. That's why he gives us the gift of faith, a gift we first receive in Baptism. Faith makes it possible for us to believe all of God's revelation.

I might have a hard time believing that my oil change really will be finished in an hour, but *I do believe* that Jesus is present in the Eucharist and that my heavenly Father is watching over me and providing for my needs. That's what faith can do.

Seeing Is Believing

We perceive the world through our senses; and of all the senses, sight is often considered the most powerful. The expression "seeing is believing" certainly holds true for many individuals. The fact that the Father, Son, and Holy Spirit are not visible makes it very difficult to believe that they are with us.

Faith can help us clear this hurdle, but we shouldn't rule out our natural reasoning ability. Without giving it too much thought, we believe in many things that we can't see. Consider air and electricity, for example. Even though we can't see them, we believe they exist. We do so primarily through the use of our intellect. At some point, probably in school, we learned that these entities exist, and we believed what our teachers told us. In these cases, our head knowledge is good enough.

A practical example comes to mind. When Eileen and I were engaged, I planned a surprise party for her thirtieth birthday. Preparation was relatively easy because I was living alone in the condo that would be our future home together, and so I could decorate without tipping off Eileen. I left the rest up to Eileen's family. My plan was to invite her out to dinner but make a quick stop at the condo to show her the new dining room table that had been delivered that day.

As we entered the door and headed up the stairs, I couldn't hear a sound. I knew (in my head) that the condo was packed with nearly forty people, but my senses told me otherwise. I couldn't see or hear the guests, but I believed that they were present.

There are times when I can absolutely feel God's presence, but more often than not, I have to rely on my intellect. I might not feel him, I might not see him, but I know that he's with me, and I behave accordingly.

When you struggle to feel God's presence, I recommend that you say, "Lord, I believe that you are here with me," and give your heart a little time to catch up with your head.

Ultimately, knowing that God is with you is more important than feeling his presence. Feelings can come and go, but the truth of God's constant presence will never change.

> As the mountains are round about Jerusalem,
>   so the LORD is round about his people,
>   from this time forth and for evermore. (Psalm 125:2)

Looking Back, Looking Ahead

As we prepare to move on to the next chapter, let's spend some time with Jesus in prayer. You can't see him and you might not feel him, but you know by faith that he exists and is present in your life. By addressing him in prayer, you put your faith into practice and confirm that you believe in his presence.

Your prayer can be as simple as telling him you know that he's with you and asking him to help you trust him more. Don't be discouraged if it feels a little unnatural at first. The more you speak to him, the easier it becomes.

We're about to discuss the third fact that we must know about God: even though it might not seem like it at times, he is bigger than any problem we will ever face.

· ·

Lord Jesus, I praise and worship you. Thank you for entering our world and redeeming us by your death on the cross.

I know that you promised to remain with us always, and I believe that you will do just that. Help me remember to call on the Holy Spirit throughout the day. Please lead me to a deeper relationship with the Father, and increase my desire to do his will.

Thank you, Lord. I love you. Amen.

CHAPTER 3

God Is Bigger Than Your Problems

In the world you have tribulation; but be of good cheer, I have overcome the world.

—**John 16:33**

Jesus never tried to deny the fact that life has its share of difficulties. Even becoming one of his followers and surrendering your life to him don't provide immunity from trials and tribulations.

Despite the fact that we will encounter problems and suffering, we should never forget that our problems are no match for God. If our problems seem too big to handle, then our God has become too small. In this chapter, we'll look at the power of the one true God and examine just why he is referred to as almighty.

Once you realize that your abilities are limited (which seems to happen every day, doesn't it?), it's easy for fear or frustration to set in. I have a tendency to be controlling, and so I can slip into panic mode in a matter of minutes. What saves me every time is the knowledge that, even though my problems are too big for me, they aren't too big for God. Here's a practical example from the not-too-distant past.

In September of 2016, I approached the management of Holy Spirit Radio in Philadelphia and presented my vision for a new and refreshing Catholic morning show. They liked the idea, and after several meetings and brainstorming sessions, *Spirit in the Morning* went live on October 10, 2016. Along with my cohost, Dave Parker, I began a two-year run presenting top Catholic guests and contemporary Christian music.

Eventually, I would become comfortable dealing with the challenges of live radio, but it wasn't that way in the beginning. To say that I didn't know what I was doing would be an understatement. Dave Parker was a good friend and a great cohost, but he only knew a little more than I did about the ins and outs of live radio. So how did we survive?

God sent someone to help, as he so often does. Frank Eliason arrived on the scene to assume the role of operations manager for the station. He had been involved in the station, working remotely, for several years. Now he was a hands-on part of the daily studio operations. And even though he had minimal radio experience, his capacity to learn and excel under pressure was remarkable.

No matter what challenge we threw at him, Frank was able to handle it. Often working under incredible pressure, he never seemed fazed by anything. In addition to keeping us on the air (no exaggeration), Frank was responsible for countless equipment upgrades and innovative programming ideas. In a word, Frank Eliason was a genius.

As time went on, I was able to relax and concentrate on my hosting duties, knowing that Frank was there to handle any crisis that popped up. I no longer worried about everything that might go wrong. Instead, I focused on being the best radio host I could be. If a technical issue arose, Frank would handle it. Knowing that I had a "Frank" standing by made any unexpected problem look much smaller.

How Big Is God?

If you want to get an idea of God's power, the Bible is a great place to start. Over and over again, throughout the Old and New Testaments, we see evidence of God's power over the enemies of his people and the forces of nature. These examples of his power help give us the confidence we need to face life's challenges without fear. The bigger our God, the smaller our problems.

In the Beginning . . .

There's no better place to begin than in the beginning: the Book of Genesis, chapter 1, verse 1. Our God is so big that his greatness is evident from the first words of Sacred Scripture:

> In the beginning God created the heavens and the earth. The earth was without form and void, and darkness was upon the face of the deep; and the Spirit of God was

moving over the face of the waters.
And God said, "Let there be light"; and there was light.
(Genesis 1:1-3)

The idea of creating something out of nothing is a tough concept to grasp, and for good reason. It's impossible for a human being to do. Yes, a painter can create a beautiful portrait, but he must make use of brushes, paint, and canvas. In a similar way, a composer cannot write a song without using musical notes, and contractors can't build new houses without using preexisting materials and tools. Only God can create something out of nothing.

In addition to giving us a glimpse into the enormity of God's creative power, the first three verses of the Bible force us to confront an extremely challenging concept. In order for God to create the heavens and the earth at the beginning of time, he had to exist prior to that time. In other words, there was never a time when God did not exist. He had no beginning and will have no end. He simply is, always was, and always will be.

Rather than trying to understand a concept beyond human reasoning, I recommend that you accept it as an illustration of his awesome power. He always existed, operates outside of time, and created light—and everything else—simply by speaking the words.

When faced with a major problem, I frequently meditate on the creation story, borrowing the words of the prophet Jeremiah: "Ah Lord GOD! It is you who have made the heavens and the earth by your great power and by your outstretched arm! Nothing is too hard for you" (Jeremiah 32:17).

I've had many days when my problems seemed too hard to solve. How about you? Fortunately, we have a heavenly Father for whom nothing is too hard. Keep that in mind whenever you start to feel hopeless. Whatever it is, God can handle it.

At War with Giants

Have you ever come face-to-face with a giant problem? I know I have: COVID-19, unemployment, loneliness, serious illness, and so on. Your problems may differ from mine, but I'm sure you've encountered your share of seemingly insurmountable ones. It's quite possible that you are staring at one right now.

David knew what it was like to stand face-to-face with a giant. He also knew the confidence that came from going into battle under the protection of almighty God. Let's take a closer look at his personal encounter with the giant Goliath.

The Philistines were a constant thorn in the side of the Israelites. In fact, their armies clashed on several occasions. The First Book of Samuel documents their most notable battle (see 1 Samuel 17). A valley lay between the two armies, as they faced each other on opposite hills. Suddenly, Goliath, who stood nine feet tall, issued a challenge to Israel's army:

> "Why have you come out to draw up for battle? Am I not a Philis'tine, and are you not servants of Saul? Choose a man for yourselves, and let him come down to me. If he is able to fight with me and kill me, then we will be your servants; but if I prevail against him and kill him, then you shall be our servants and serve us." (17:8-9)

Upon hearing the taunts of Goliath, the Bible tells us, King Saul and the Israelites were "dismayed and greatly afraid" (1 Samuel 17:11). As a result, they failed to respond to his challenge, and for forty days, Goliath continued to strut defiantly before the Israelite army. Finally, someone did step up and express his willingness to accept the giant's challenge.

David, the youngest son of a man named Jesse, heard the taunts of Goliath. Offended that the Philistine would "defy the armies of the living God" and terrorize the soldiers, David approached King Saul with a courageous offer: "Let no man's heart fail because of him; your servant will go and fight with this Philis'tine" (1 Samuel 17:26, 32).

Citing David's young age and lack of experience, the king rejected the offer. It certainly makes sense, doesn't it? If you're going to choose one man to square off against a giant warrior, you would pick someone powerful, not a young man whose main work experience was taking care of his father's sheep. But David persisted:

"Your servant used to keep sheep for his father; and when there came a lion, or a bear, and took a lamb from the flock, I went after him and struck him and delivered it out of his mouth; and if he arose against me, I caught him by his beard, and struck him and killed him. Your servant has killed both lions and bears; and this uncircumcised Philis'tine shall be like one of them, seeing he has defied the armies of the living God." And David said, "The Lord who delivered me from the paw of the lion and from the paw of the

bear, will deliver me from the hand of this Philis'tine."
(1 Samuel 17:34-37)

The king finally relented and sent the youthful warrior into battle. Insulted by the Israelite army's representative and the fact that David's weapon of choice was a slingshot, Goliath let loose with a barrage of threats. David confidently replied with words that can strengthen us when facing our own giants:

> "You come to me with a sword and with a spear and with a javelin; but I come to you in the name of the LORD of hosts, the God of the armies of Israel, whom you have defied. This day the LORD will deliver you into my hand, and I will strike you down, and cut off your head; and I will give the dead bodies of the host of the Philis'tines this day to the birds of the air and to the wild beasts of the earth; that all the earth may know that there is a God in Israel, and that all this assembly may know that the LORD saves not with sword and spear; for the battle is the LORD's and he will give you into our hand." (1 Samuel 17:45-47)

With the help of the Lord, David was able to slay Goliath and emerge victorious. On seeing the death of their mighty warrior, the Philistine army turned and fled.

That's what happens when you go into battle with God on your side. He hasn't lost a battle yet. Keep this in mind as you look up at your giants today. You may feel outmatched by the enormity of your problems, but you have God on your side.

Asleep on a Cushion

Sleeping in the midst of a raging storm is a skill I haven't mastered. Whether we're speaking about a literal storm, with thunder and lightning, or a figurative one, such as a health crisis, the ability to relax can seem unimaginable—unless you happen to be Jesus.

If you're looking for an illustration of the Lord's power, an incident that took place on the Sea of Galilee two thousand years ago delivers in a big way. No matter how many times I read it, I learn something new each time. The story of the storm at sea (see Mark 4:35-41) is so powerful that I always find a way to work it into my talks or parish missions. If we understand what's taking place here and with whom we're dealing, we'll find it difficult to panic when problems arise in our life.

The story begins one evening, when Jesus said to his disciples, "Let us go across to the other side" (Mark 4:35). With that, they all got in the boat and proceeded across the Sea of Galilee. Suddenly a great storm arose, and the boat was beginning to fill with water. Uh-oh. Maybe Jesus should have checked the weather report before he came up with this idea.

On the other hand, maybe this sailing expedition was designed to teach his followers (that's us!) an important lesson. It's a lesson best taught not on dry land or in a classroom but in the middle of a raging storm.

Immediately after telling us about the storm, Mark delivers my favorite detail: Jesus was asleep on a cushion in the stern. How could Jesus sleep during a raging storm? Probably because he knew that there was nothing to fear. As we'll soon discover, he was bigger than the storm, and he knew it.

The disciples hadn't received the memo. They were terrified, as evidenced by their frightened words. Waking Jesus, they cried out, "Teacher, do you not care if we perish?" (Mark 4:38).

The first thing I want to point out is that the disciples did the right thing by waking Jesus. I would strongly encourage you to follow their lead and turn to Jesus whenever you face a crisis. Despite the fact that their actions were right on the money, however, their words reveal glaring deficiencies in their thinking.

First, they made the same mistake that many of us do when facing a crisis. *They assumed Jesus didn't care.* Just because Jesus appears to be silent—or sleeping—in the middle of your crisis doesn't mean that he doesn't care about you. He's totally in control and is right beside you.

Second, *they assumed that the storm was going to kill them.* We frequently fall into this trap as our fears overwhelm us. Had the disciples listened to Jesus before they got in the boat ("Let us go across to the other side"—Mark 4:35) they would have realized that they were going to make it to the other side.

Did you notice that the disciples accused Jesus of not caring but never asked him to calm the storm? Somehow it did not occur to them that he could fix the problem. And so he showed them his power: "And he awoke and rebuked the wind, and said to the sea, 'Peace! Be still!' And the wind ceased, and there was a great calm" (Mark 4:39).

Just like that, the storm ceased, and there was a great calm. All it took was a command from the Lord. Filled with awe, the disciples asked, "Who then is this, that even wind and sea obey him?" (Mark 4:41).

It's a great question, and one that we should ask ourselves when faced with an unsolvable problem. Who is he? He's the God of the universe, who is bigger and more powerful than any crisis we will ever face.

Obstacles

Opening the Bible to read about God's mighty deeds is a great way to build confidence in his ability to handle even your most difficult problem. I highly recommend that you do this on a regular basis because the Bible is filled with stories of God's power.

If you're looking for a good place to start, consider the miracles of Jesus. Beginning with the changing of water to wine at Cana (see John 2), Jesus performed several documented miracles as proof of his divinity. Many Bibles include a complete list, typically in the index, and you can also do an internet search for "miracles of Jesus."

Miracles aside, the fact remains that several common obstacles can diminish our belief in God's power. Let's look at a few of them.

"I'm Too Weak!"

Who among us hasn't felt this way at times? When confronted with life's unexpected challenges, it's easy to feel helpless.

Rather than trying to fight it and assuming an "I can do anything" attitude, I suggest that you embrace your weakness. Yes, you heard that right. You are weak, I am weak, everyone who has ever lived is weak—and that's okay.

We live in a world that constantly emphasizes the importance of being strong, but the idea of self-contained strength isn't healthy. It's not realistic either. Whom are we trying to kid? None of us are strong enough to face the challenges of life alone. Pretending that we are will eventually plunge us into discouragement or despair. So how should we proceed?

St. Paul offers great advice in his second letter to the people of Corinth. Struggling with an unspecified "thorn . . . in the flesh" (2 Corinthians 12:7), Paul prayed three times for God to take it away. Instead of granting the request, the Lord responded, "My grace is sufficient for you, for my power is made perfect in weakness" (12:9).

Did you catch that? The power of God is made *perfect* in weakness. The weaker you are, the more powerfully the Lord can work in your life. Paul's response indicates a clear understanding of that concept and a newfound willingness to embrace the very weakness he asked God to take away:

> I will all the more gladly boast of my weaknesses, that the power of Christ may rest upon me. For the sake of Christ, then, I am content with weaknesses, insults, hardships, persecutions, and calamities; for when I am weak, then I am strong. (2 Corinthians 12:9-10)

Don't dwell on the fact that you are weak. Instead, accept that fact as a reminder to rely on the strength of God. Just like Paul, when you are weak, you are strong.

"It Isn't Possible"

Despite the fact that Scripture tells us that all things are possible for God (see Luke 1:37), we frequently allow ourselves to be overwhelmed by what we perceive to be an impossible problem. Whenever we take on this mindset, God seems to become a little less powerful. Somehow we need to come up with a way to stop dwelling on the enormity of the mountain and focus on the One who is infinitely larger than the mountain.

When my wife was pregnant with our twins, Mary and Elizabeth, the doctors told us that the girls had only a 10-percent chance of being born alive. The girls did survive and are healthy young ladies today, thanks to the Lord's mercy and countless prayers. As I look back, I can see clear-cut evidence of God's power at work.

While we were going through it, however, the problem seemed bigger than almighty God. Knowing that my thinking was off, I began to pray in a different way. My prayer sounded something like this: "Lord, I'm having trouble believing that you can perform a miracle and allow the girls to be born alive. The doctors are painting a very grim picture. I know in my head that you can do all things, but I'm having troubling believing it right now. No matter how this turns out, I need to believe that you can heal them. Please help me believe."

It didn't take much time for God to answer my prayer. In spite of the evidence to the contrary, I started to truly believe that God could pull this off. As a result, I was able to confidently pray for a miraculous healing. And that's exactly what happened.

When the world tells you that something is impossible, turn to God and ask him to help you believe that all things are possible for him. Take it from me; he loves answering that prayer.

Focusing on the Wrong Thing

Sometimes we can lose sight of God's power simply by focusing on the wrong thing. Too much time dwelling on the problem will take away time that could be used to focus on God and his power. Because the human brain can only focus on one thought at a time, I can think either about God or about my problem.

If I choose to think about God and his power, chances are good that I will feel confident and secure about what lies ahead. Thinking about the gory details and worst-case scenarios associated with my crisis du jour, on the other hand, will tend to increase my anxiety and possibly lead me to despair.

St. Peter knew what it was like to lose his focus. In one of the more widely known incidents in the Bible (detailed in Matthew 14:22-35), he had the chance to accomplish a feat most people would think of as impossible: walking on water. The incident took place while Peter and the disciples were crossing the Sea of Galilee in a boat. As they battled the wind, Jesus came toward them, walking on the water.

Seeing Jesus, the disciples were terrified, thinking that he was a ghost. Peter, on the other hand, called out to Jesus and asked to be invited to walk on the water too. After getting the go-ahead from the Lord, Peter stepped out of the boat and began to walk. It was a true miracle!

But then Peter saw the strength of the wind, and he began to sink. In order to look at the storm, Peter had taken his eyes off Jesus, and that's when the trouble started. Once he refocused on Jesus, all was well.

I want to alert you to a surprising manifestation of this common obstacle. Believe it or not, we sometimes cause this problem by the way we pray. As an example, suppose you notice an unusual lump on your neck one day. Your doctor believes that it is an enlarged lymph node and sends you for a biopsy to determine if you are suffering from lymphoma. Believing in the power of prayer, you decide to pray about it.

You could say something like "Lord, you can do all things. Please let the biopsy be negative" or "Please don't let me have cancer." You could also pray in a more specific way, such as, "Lord, please don't let me have cancer. If I do, I might need to have chemotherapy, and my hair may fall out. And what if the treatment makes me so sick that I start to lose weight and have to take time off from work? They might fire me, and then I won't be able to pay my bills. We could end up homeless. If this is cancer, I could die. If that happens, what will my children do? Oh, please, Lord. Please, please, please, don't let this turn out bad. I won't be able to handle it."

Do you see how the second way of praying could cause you to lose confidence in God and fear the possibility of a potentially life-threatening, but still undiagnosed, disease? By all means, bring your concerns to God, but sometimes it's better to gloss over some of the details. God really does know what you mean. Instead of spending all your prayer time talking to God about how big your problems are, spend time talking to your problems about how big your God is.

> Have you not known? Have you not heard?
> The LORD is the everlasting God,
>   the Creator of the ends of the earth.
> He does not faint or grow weary,
>   his understanding is unsearchable.
> He gives power to the faint,
>   and to him who has no might he increases strength.
> (Isaiah 40:28-29)

Looking Back, Looking Ahead

Although it's impossible to fully grasp the power of God, it is possible to acquire some degree of understanding. The material we covered in this chapter will give you a good place to start, but it is not exhaustive by any means. I encourage you to keep looking for signs in Scripture and in the world of God's ability to do all things. The more we understand what he can do, the less afraid we will be when confronted with the problems of life.

God loves you, God is with you, and God is bigger than your problems. These concepts are so important that failing to grasp them will make it impossible to move forward in your relationship with God.

In this first part of this book, we looked at numerous examples illustrating God's unconditional love, omnipresence, and omnipotence. But learning from a book that he loves you, is with you, and is bigger than your problems is only part of what it takes to know God. In order to really know him, you have to encounter him every day. As we get ready to move on to the next section and explore ways to love God, let's continue our lifelong journey with God by addressing him directly.

. . . .

Heavenly Father, when I think about your awesome works throughout the ages, I am overcome with gratitude. You created the entire universe and hold it in the palm of your hand, but you are never too busy for me. Through Jesus I am able to call you Father. Wow!

Please help me better understand how much you love me. Help me recognize your presence at all times and understand just how powerful you really are. Send your Holy Spirit to awaken me to your powerful presence and allow me to feel your love.

I ask this in Jesus' name. Amen.

PART TWO

LOVING GOD

You shall love the LORD your God with all your heart, and with all your soul, and with all your might.

—Deuteronomy 6:5

As a prelude to entering into a loving relationship with God, we need to know some important facts about him: who he is and that he loves us, he is with us, and he is bigger than our problems. This is the foundational knowledge that we covered in the first three chapters. If we combine that basic knowledge with prayer—spending time in his presence—we become better equipped to move on to the next phase of the journey, that of entering more deeply into a loving relationship with him.

So how exactly do we do that? How do we love God? We have established that love isn't a feeling but a conscious decision. Loving God begins with the decision to love him, but there is more to it than that. In the next three chapters, we are going to discuss how to love God with our attitude, behavior, and commitment. I call this the ABCs of loving God.

Attitude (A): All our love for God begins in the mind, with our thoughts and desires. When faced with unpleasant circumstances, for example, we can choose to accept them without complaining.

Behavior (B): We also love God through our behavior. This includes prayer, serving others, reading Scripture, receiving the sacraments, and so forth.

Commitment (C): We also express our love for God by making a commitment to him. No matter what happens, we resolve, to the best of our ability, to be faithful.

Before we get into the nitty-gritty of loving God, I have some good news for you. By picking up this book and reading about God in the first three chapters, you have already started to love him. The fact that you care enough about God to read about growing closer to him is, in itself, an act of love.

Pretty cool, isn't it? You have already started to love God. Let's continue the discussion.

CHAPTER 4

Loving with Your Mind

And he said to him, "You shall love the Lord your God with all your heart, and with all your soul, and with all your mind."
—Matthew 22:37

Loving God with your entire mind requires an act of the will: we must make a conscious decision to put God first. Whenever we choose to exercise our free will and commit to loving God, we are already loving him. Actions will flow from that decision, of course, but we shouldn't downplay the importance of our thoughts and intentions.

We'll focus on actions in the next chapter; here let's look at how we love God with our thoughts and desires. Why start here? Because it's essential that we love him with our hearts and minds first; otherwise, our words and deeds—our actions—can be meaningless rituals.

Singling out the Pharisees, who frequently just went through the motions of faith, Jesus cited the prophet Isaiah. His words should serve as a warning for each of us:

"You hypocrites! Well did Isaiah prophesy of you, when he said:

'This people honors me with their lips,
but their heart is far from me;
in vain do they worship me,
teaching as doctrines the precepts of men.'" (Matthew 15:7-9; see Isaiah 29:13)

Before you can love God with your words and actions, you must first love him with your mind and heart. Let's take a closer look at how we can do that.

Surrender

The word "surrender" generally has a negative connotation. Many view it as a sign of weakness or defeat. In a world that emphasizes achievement and self-sufficiency, surrendering is typically the last thing we want to do. After all, many think that to surrender is to quit—and who wants to be a quitter?

When it comes to our relationship with God, however, one of the best things we can do is surrender to his will. When we decide to do things his way instead of our way, we show our love for him.

Surrendering to God begins with an act of the will. In other words, I make a conscious decision to yield control of my life, as well as the lives of my loved ones, to him. Charles de Foucauld's Prayer of Abandonment captures what such surrender looks like.

Father,
I abandon myself into your hands;
do with me what you will.
Whatever you may do, I thank you:
I am ready for all, I accept all.

Let only your will be done in me,
and in all your creatures—
I wish no more than this, O Lord.

Into your hands I commend my soul:
I offer it to you with all the love of my heart,
for I love you, Lord, and so need to give myself,
to surrender myself into your hands without reserve,
and with boundless confidence,
for you are my Father. [1]

When we pray these words, we deliberately choose to place our lives in God's hands. In doing so, we imitate Jesus, whose entire life was dedicated to doing the will of the Father. "For I have come down from heaven, not to do my own will, but the will of him who sent me" (John 6:38).

Nowhere is Jesus' abandonment more evident than on the night before he died. About to face an excruciatingly painful death, Jesus clearly and deliberately surrendered his own will to the will of his Father. He didn't do it because he was afraid or even because it was the right thing to do. Jesus surrendered to the Father's will out of love.

> And going a little farther he fell on his face and prayed, "My Father, if it be possible, let this chalice pass from me; nevertheless, not as I will, but as thou will." (Matthew 26:39)

So what happens after we surrender to God's will? Is it just a matter of making the decision, saying the words, and moving on with life? Not at all. Those things are necessary, but there's more for us to do.

Once I tell God that I surrender my life into his hands, I should be prepared to respond appropriately when events begin to unfold. I told him that he was in charge—and I hope I meant it—and so I should be willing to accept whatever happens to me without complaining.

I know. Those last two words trip me up frequently, but I'm working on it.

When I need some inspiration, I like to look at the words of Job after he lost his family and possessions. "Naked I came from my mother's womb, and naked shall I return; the LORD gave, and the LORD has taken away; blessed be the name of the LORD" (Job 1:21). Job obviously understood the meaning of surrender and detachment.

A Heart in the Right Place

I'm sure you've heard it said that someone's "heart was in the right place." We typically use this expression when referring to a person whose actions are questionable but whose motives are good. Or to a person whose efforts to accomplish something ended in failure or disappointment. The world may only look at the end product, but God always rewards our good motives.

King David wanted to build a temple to honor the Lord, but God had other plans. God did want the temple to be built, but he didn't want David to do the building. Even though he referred to David as "a man after my heart" (Acts 13:22; see 1 Samuel 13:14), God rejected his offer to build a temple, for David had "shed much blood and . . . waged great wars" (1 Chronicles 22:8).

And so the Lord chose David's son, Solomon, a man of peace, to build the temple. Although he was disappointed, David obeyed God. He made all the preparations but did not actually build the temple.

In reflecting on his father's unfulfilled dream, Solomon teaches us something about the importance God places on the motives of our hearts and minds:

> Now it was in the heart of David my father to build a house for the name of the LORD, the God of Israel. But the LORD said to David my father, "Whereas it was in your heart to build a house for my name, you did well that it was in your heart." (2 Chronicles 6:7-8)

David's desire to build the temple was more important to God than the actual construction. Through that desire and subsequent obedience, David showed his love for God without doing this great thing.

Even If . . .

It was a very dark time for the Jewish people, as recorded in the Book of Daniel. The kingdom of Judah had fallen, and the temple, built by Solomon, had been destroyed. Nebuchadnezzar, the conquering king, decided to move some of the up-and-coming young leaders to Babylon in order to assimilate them into Babylonian culture.

Daniel, Hananiah, Mishael, and Azariah were among those taken into captivity. They were given the Babylonian names of Belteshazzar, Shadrach, Meshach, and Abednego. They were to be trained for three years, after which they would enter the royal service.

The four young men were being groomed for greatness, but they ran into difficulty. They were devout Jews, unwilling to abandon their dietary practices and defile themselves by eating unclean food. Their internal resolve to remain faithful to the Lord was nothing less than an act of love for him. Fortunately, through the cooperation of their attendant, who supplied them with vegetables and water, they were able to get around this obstacle and remain in the king's good graces. Unfortunately, this reprieve didn't last.

King Nebuchadnezzar had his workers construct a ninety-foot gold statue and commanded everyone to bow down and worship it. Anyone who refused to obey would be cast into a blazing hot furnace. Choosing to remain faithful to the Lord, Shadrach, Meshach, and Abednego were not about to bow down to a golden idol. When the king discovered that the young men refused to worship the statue, he flew into a rage. Ordering the men to appear before him, he gave them one last chance to save themselves by obeying his command.

> Shad'rach, Me'shach, and Abed'nego answered the king, "O Nebuchadnez'zar, we have no need to answer you in this matter. If it be so, our God whom we serve is able to deliver us from the burning fiery furnace; and he will deliver us out of your hand, O king. But if not, be it known to you, O king, that we will not serve your gods or worship the golden image which you have set up." (Daniel 3:16-18)

The three men didn't know for sure that God would save them from meeting their death in the furnace, but they certainly knew that he was able to. Remember what we discussed in the last chapter—that God is bigger than our problems? Shadrach, Meshach, and Abednego were well aware of that fact. Now, here's what makes their story so powerful: *even if* the Lord chose not to spare them, they would still not abandon him by worshiping a false god.

That determination in the face of a very real threat was an act of love for God. They made up their minds that they would not disrespect the Lord, even if it cost them their lives. They showed their love for him even before they had to step into the furnace. In the end, their lives were spared, and King Nebuchadnezzar praised the one true God.

Parting Words

After I graduated from college, I was hired by the Department of Defense as a computer specialist. My specific area of responsibility was computer security. My supervisor, Roy, and I were responsible for protecting the data on our numerous computer systems.

Since I was fresh out of college and new to the job, I pretty much did what I was told. Whenever I was unsure or had to make a decision, Roy was there to help me. There were only two of us, and so I sometimes filled in for him when he was in a meeting or out of the office for the day.

I was only on the job for a few months when Roy informed me that he would be taking a two-week vacation and leaving me in charge. This was a big responsibility—we managed military systems—and I was still the new guy, but Roy made sure I was well taken care of during his absence. He wrote up a detailed set of instructions and a lengthy to-do list. Even though I was still nervous, I felt better prepared to handle whatever came my way.

As Jesus prepared to give up his life on the cross, he left his followers with a to-do list that is as relevant today as it was then. Amazingly, he distilled this detailed set of instructions into a single sentence. Don't be fooled by the familiar words or the comforting tone. These simple words are, in essence, an instruction manual for loving God and living the Christian life: "Let not your hearts be troubled; believe in God, believe also in me" (John 14:1).

Take a close look at what Jesus is saying. This sentence contains three imperatives we should not ignore. When Jesus says, "Let not" and then "believe" (twice), he isn't urging us to feel a certain way. He isn't giving us a pat on the back and telling us to hang in there. Jesus is commanding us to do something. Because his command involves the mind and not a physical activity, however, it's easy to miss his call to action. Let's take a closer look.

How can I prevent my heart from being troubled? Initially, it seems as if Jesus is asking me to do the impossible and control my emotions. That isn't possible, however, because we can't control the way we feel (although we can control the way we behave). We can assume, therefore, that there's something more to his statement. After all, he would never ask us to do the impossible.

The key to letting your heart be untroubled lies in what Jesus said next. In order to "untrouble" our heart, we must believe in God, and we must believe in Jesus.

Now, while this whole believing thing sounds simple, there's more to it than just recognizing the existence of Jesus and his Father. The original Greek manuscript of John's Gospel offers a different shade of meaning for the word commonly translated as "believe. " It uses the word *pisteuo,* which means "to place confidence in" or "to trust." Once we make the decision to place our confidence in Jesus and trust that what he's saying is true, our hearts start to become less troubled.

But we must *decide*. Note the deliberate involvement of the mind.

When we believe what Jesus told us about the Father and his provision for our lives, our stress level begins to decrease. And you know what else? This deliberate choice to trust the Father and the Son, even in the midst of a storm, is an act of love.

Can you still make this choice if you're scared to death? Absolutely. And here's something to consider: when you are filled with fear and still make the choice to trust God, not only are you showing your love for him, but you're actually expressing greater love than if you did it when you were totally at peace.

Learning to Ponder

No discussion of loving God with our minds would be complete without addressing meditation, or mental prayer. Don't let the word intimidate you. "Meditation" simply means thinking attentively about God, or something pertaining to him, in order to deepen our faith. Whenever we do this, we perform an act of love. Sometimes referred to as pondering, this practice of consciously dwelling on God and his actions was one of the specialties of Mary, the mother of Jesus.

The story of the Annunciation in the Gospel of Luke brings Mary's experience of pondering, or meditation, to light. The angel Gabriel appeared to Mary and informed her that she had been chosen for a special role: to be the mother of the Messiah.

> And he came to her and said, "Hail, full of grace, the Lord is with you!" But she was greatly troubled at the saying, and considered in her mind what sort of greeting this might be. (Luke 1:28-29)

As soon as the angel greeted her, Mary began to think about the implications of his visit. Based on her knowledge of the Hebrew Scriptures, she knew that angels didn't visit people just to say, "Hi." Mary knew something big was up, and she sought to discern what it could be. This is the first time the Bible records Mary pondering the mysteries of God. It isn't the last.

When Jesus was born, an angel of the Lord announced the good news to shepherds watching their flock (see Luke 2:9-11). Wanting to see for themselves, they decided to travel to Bethlehem.

> And they went with haste, and found Mary and Joseph, and the baby lying in a manger. And when they saw it they made known the saying which had been told them concerning this child; and all who heard it wondered at what the shepherds told them. But Mary kept all these things, pondering them in her heart. (2:16-19)

The shepherds made known what the angel told them about Jesus, and everyone who heard their words wondered—"marveled" or "admired," in the original Greek—at what the angel said. Mary *kept all these things* in her mind so that she wouldn't forget, as the Greek manuscript makes clear. She pondered them. Wanting to enter more deeply into her relationship with God and his Son, she would continue to meditate on what the angel revealed to the shepherds.

Finally, when Jesus was twelve years old, Mary and Joseph left him behind in Jerusalem when they journeyed back to Nazareth. Realizing their mistake, the frantic parents returned to

Jerusalem and, after searching for three days, found Jesus in the Temple, sitting among the teachers. Once again, faced with a confusing set of circumstances, Mary pondered.

> And when they saw him they were astonished; and his mother said to him, "Son, why have you treated us so? Behold, your father and I have been looking for you anxiously." And he said to them, "How is it that you sought me? Did you not know that I must be in my Father's house?" And they did not understand the saying which he spoke to them. And he went down with them and came to Nazareth, and was obedient to them; and his mother kept all these things in her heart. (Luke 2:48-51)

Mary certainly expressed her love from God through her words and actions, but she also loved him with her mind. By choosing to think about him, to ponder his attributes and greatness, we can do the same.

Obstacles

There are several obstacles that can block us from loving God with our mind. We could argue that our fast-paced and technology-driven world fuels these obstacles, but similar challenges have always been around. For centuries people have had to struggle to find time for meditation, drown out the noise of the world, and look past the instant gratification promised by materialism.

Let's look at a few of these challenges and explore ways to take back control of our minds.

Not Enough Time

One of the more memorable individuals from my software development days was a man named Lou. Our mutual dislike of the deadlines and pressure of the job helped us become friends almost as soon as we met. Lou was about ten years older than I and often drew on his prior work experiences when trying to make a point. He passed away over a decade ago, but many of these "Lou-isms" are permanently etched in my memory.

One of my favorites involves the time he questioned his boss on a proposed solution to a technical problem. The supervisor's response was short and to the point: "We don't pay you to think; we pay you to work. Just do it!"

The world encourages the "just do it" mentality, and to be fair, that might be the right approach when we're under pressure: don't waste time thinking; just get busy and start working. This mindset, however, doesn't carry over when it comes to meditation. The "just do it" approach, with its emphasis on frenetic activity, seriously undermines the value of sitting quietly with Jesus or the Father or the Holy Spirit.

Choosing to be still and spend time with the Lord is a good thing. Jesus commended Mary of Bethany for sitting at his feet and listening to his teaching (see Luke 10:38-42). He invited Peter, James, and John to keep him company in the Garden of Gethsemane (see Matthew 26:36-37; Mark 14:32-33). No matter what anyone tries to tell you, time spent attentively reflecting on the words or presence of the Lord is *always* time well spent.

Too Much Noise

We live in a noisy world. No matter where we go, the noise seems to follow. In order to hear God speak and then reflect on his words, we must find a way to escape from the noise.

This must be a deliberate choice on our part. As Jesus said, "Go into your room and shut the door and pray to your Father who is in secret" (Matthew 6:6). Mark's Gospel records that Jesus "rose and went out to a lonely place, and there he prayed" (1:35). The message for us? Find a quiet place, and spend time with God.

Thinking about Worldly Things

It's easy for me to think about worldly things. I've done so ever since I was a small child, and I'm really good at it! Thinking about God, heaven, and other spiritual things is a little more difficult.

John warns against loving the world or the things of the world (see 1 John 2:15), but sometimes that's easier said than done. Is there a solution?

Fortunately, Jesus knew we would struggle in this area. He sent the Holy Spirit to dwell in us so that we can think with "the mind of Christ" (1 Corinthians 2:16). Tapping into the power of the Spirit will help us rise above the desire to dwell on worldly things and help us meditate instead on the invisible kingdom. The simple invitation "Come, Holy Spirit" is a great way to lift our minds to heavenly things.

When the days for his being taken up were fulfilled, he resolutely determined to journey to Jerusalem. (Luke 9:51, NABRE)

Looking Back, Looking Ahead

As we have discussed, loving God is often a matter of attitude. Before we can love him with our actions, we must first love him with our thoughts and our will. Any time spent reflecting on him and the mysteries of his kingdom is time spent loving him.

In the next chapter, we'll look at how we can express our love for God through our behavior. There is overlapping between loving God with the mind and loving him through our actions, but there are differences as well. Now that we've learned the importance of attitude, let's take the next step and learn to love God not only with our minds but with our bodies as well.

• •

Dear Holy Spirit, I give you permission to inspire all my thoughts, words, and actions. Please help me think with the mind of Jesus and focus more on the invisible kingdom of God than on the visible world. Strengthen my will so that I can resist the distractions around me and choose instead to "waste time" by reflecting on the mysteries of God.

I ask this in Jesus' name. Amen.

CHAPTER 5

Actions Speak Louder Than Words

Little children, let us not love in word or speech but in deed and in truth.

—1 John 3:18

Here's something to consider: all our actions begin with thoughts, but not all our thoughts result in actions.

In the last chapter, we explored many ways we can love God through the use of our intellect—our thoughts, will, and attitude. But loving God shouldn't end there. At some point, love has to be expressed in our behavior.

Before going on, I have to confess that I struggle with this all the time. I find it much easier to think about God than to do things for him. In all honesty, thinking about God requires much less effort and can make me feel really good. When we operate from this mindset, however, we're more or less going through the motions. A sincere love of God involves not only the mind but the body as well.

Let's look at an example. Suppose a husband loves his wife and thinks of her often. Several times throughout the day, he stops what he's doing and reflects on how much she means to him. He reflects on her beauty and even gets choked up as he remembers the selfless love that she demonstrates on a daily basis. The more he thinks about her, the happier it makes him.

From time to time, he'll consider potential vacation destinations that would allow his wife to get away from the daily grind and relax. Invariably, however, something comes up, and he never books the trip. When he gets home from work, there are so many distractions that he never manages to tell his wife that she's beautiful or to say, "I love you." And though he really would like to pitch in with the household chores and give his wife some much-needed relief, there always seems to be a must-see show or sporting event on TV.

Is this husband truly loving his wife as much as he could? Love begins in the mind, but it shouldn't stay there.

In the parable of the two sons (see Matthew 21:28-32), Jesus drives this point home in a memorable way. The story tells of a man who asked his two sons to go and work in the field. The first son initially said no but then changed his mind and went. The second son agreed to go but did not.

Jesus asked the priests and elders—the audience for this parable—which son obeyed the father. They said the one who initially refused but then went anyway. Jesus confirmed their answer by emphasizing that sinners were entering the kingdom of God before many of the "holy" folks.

When it comes to loving God, it's not good enough to say the right words and think the right thoughts. Ultimately, it comes down to behavior.

From Thought to Prayer

Before we go any further, let's consider prayer as action, even though we don't usually think of it as an action or behavior. Of course we can't stay locked in our prayer, in a way similar to that self-satisfied husband we just considered. We must step out to meet the needs of others. But even silent prayer involves a conscious decision and a deliberate series of steps. And because this chapter is all about loving God through our behavior, let's touch on how we can do that through prayer.

The Bible tells us that Daniel got down on his knees and prayed three times a day (see Daniel 6:10). It was a deliberate choice on his part. In order for this to happen, Daniel had to stop what he was doing (a conscious decision), get down on his knees (another deliberate choice), and offer prayers to God. Nothing about what he did was accidental. Through his thoughts, actions, and words, Daniel was expressing his love for God.

Need another example? The Bible tells us that Jesus rose early in the morning and "went out to a lonely place, and there he prayed" (Mark 1:35). Whenever I'm tempted to sleep in or skip my morning prayers, I think about the many times Jesus made a deliberate effort to communicate with his Father in prayer. It has helped me remember that if it was important to him, it should be even more important to me.

As someone who likes to be in control and get things done, I totally understand how difficult it can be to sit still and pray. I'll go ahead and say what you may be thinking: sometimes prayer feels like a waste of time. With so much to get done and so little time in which to do it, who has the time to pray?

This is hardly a new dilemma. People have been struggling with this problem for centuries. I can't think of a better illustration of this struggle than a familiar story from the Gospel of Luke (see 10:38-42).

As Jesus was traveling to Jerusalem with his disciples, he stopped at the home of his friends Martha and Mary. After welcoming him into her home, Martha became "distracted with much serving" (Luke 10:40), while Mary "sat at the Lord's feet and listened to his teaching" (10:39). Overcome by frustration and feeling used, Martha confronted Jesus. Getting right to the point, she informed him of the situation, accused him of not caring, and commanded him to fix the problem. "Lord, do you not care that my sister has left me to serve alone? Tell her then to help me" (10:40).

Much to the surprise of Martha—there's no way she could have expected this response—Jesus informed her that "Mary has chosen the good portion, which shall not be taken away from her" (Luke 10:42).

Martha was so focused on her work that she had become "anxious and troubled about many things" (Luke 10:41) and had lost sight of Jesus. She may have welcomed Jesus into her home, but Mary welcomed him into her heart. Don't be fooled by Mary's sedentary position. Even though it appeared that she was doing nothing, her act of sitting still at the feet of Jesus was a conscious and powerful act of love.

Don't Just Stand There!

Sometimes we express love for God by putting our bodies into motion, and sometimes we do it by deliberately being still. Then there are those cases when we do a little bit of both. The story of the Israelites' escape from slavery in Egypt offers a useful example (see Exodus 14).

The Israelites were on their journey when Moses—at the Lord's instruction—ordered them to "turn back" (Exodus 14:2) and set up camp in the wilderness, by the sea. We might reasonably wonder why the Lord wanted them to stop when he knew that the Egyptians would soon be in close pursuit. As we quickly learn, the Lord devised this rather unusual plan because his ultimate goal was to demonstrate his power to both Pharaoh and the Israelites. To do so, first he had to place the Israelites in a precarious situation.

We know how things unfolded. Pharaoh and his officials, having had second thoughts about letting the Israelites go, pursued them. The Israelites found themselves trapped between the Egyptian army and the Red Sea—like sitting ducks, caught between a rock and a hard place. Beginning to panic, the Israelites did what we often do when our circumstances take a turn for the worse: they looked for someone to blame.

The Israelites turned on Moses. They accused him of making them leave the "comfort" of slavery in Egypt. In an effort to calm and encourage them, Moses said,

> "Fear not, stand firm, and see the salvation of the LORD, which he will work for you today; for the Egyptians whom you see today, you shall never see again. The LORD will fight for you, and you have only to be still." (Exodus 14:13-14)

Sounds like pretty good advice to me. It's your basic let-go-and-let-God message. What better way to show confidence in God than by standing still and trusting him in the face of serious danger?

Moses was finally learning to trust God and was teaching his people to do the same. "Hey, guys! God loves you and will fight for you. Let's show him how much we love him by standing still and trusting him."

It sounds like a great course of action, but there's just one problem: it wasn't God's plan. Scripture tells us this:

> The LORD said to Moses, "Why do you cry to me? Tell the sons of Israel to go forward. Lift up your rod, and stretch out your hand over the sea and divide it, that the sons of Israel may go on dry ground through the sea." (Exodus 14:15-16)

Yes, God did want his people to sit still for a while, there in that camp, but then he wanted them to move. Once Moses and the people obeyed God and got going, things fell into place, and the Egyptians were swept away as the sea closed in on them. How do we know which course of action we should take? Follow the example of Moses, who prayed and listened to the Lord. Spend time with God in prayer every day. He'll let you know when it's time to move and when it's time to remain still. And every time you obey and follow his lead, you express your love for him.

Bearing Good Fruit

How can we be sure that we're loving God through our behavior? One of the best ways is to look at the "fruit" we produce. As you probably surmised, I'm not talking about apples and oranges but about the fruit of the Holy Spirit. According to St. Paul, "The fruit of the Spirit is love, joy, peace, patience, kindness, goodness, faithfulness, gentleness, self-control" (Galatians 5:22-23).

If we give the Spirit permission to work in our lives, we should see evidence of these fruits. Let's take a brief look at each of them.

Love. As we mentioned earlier, St. Thomas Aquinas defines love as "willing the good of another." It's not a feeling but a conscious decision. True love is self-sacrificing. It involves putting others first. It's the kind of love exhibited by Jesus when he died on the cross.

Joy. Joy is the response to the Lord's presence within us. Unlike pleasure, joy doesn't depend on external circumstances. As with love, joy is a choice. For this reason, St. Paul could tell us—even when he was under house arrest—to rejoice (see Philippians 4:4). If he can do it, we can too.

Peace. This fruit of the Spirit represents a sense of serenity, or tranquility. Peace keeps the mind untroubled, even in the face of storms and trials. Jesus gives us this fruit through his

Spirit (see John 14:27). As with joy, peace doesn't depend on the absence of conflict.

Patience. Patience is a willingness to wait on God, on circumstances, and on ourselves. In order to experience patience, we must first relinquish the desire to control our environment. Praying for an increase in this fruit often results in the introduction of a challenging person or situation into our lives.

Kindness. Best described as mercy in action, the fruit of kindness flows from unconditional love. Kindness often manifests itself as the willingness to give someone another chance. God treats us with kindness, and he expects us to treat others the same way.

Goodness. Goodness involves avoiding sin and doing what is right—in other words, practicing God-like behavior. Our fallen human nature makes it difficult to behave in this way, but we can do it with the help of the Holy Spirit.

Faithfulness. God always keeps his promises, and we can too. We often fall short here, even when we have the best of intentions. The Holy Spirit will assist us if we let him.

Gentleness. While not typically associated with power, gentleness is essentially power under control. Sometimes referred to as meekness, gentleness involves channeling our power and using it for good. Jesus displayed this fruit frequently over the course of his life.

Self-control. Because we are material creatures with a fallen human nature, we find it difficult to control our passions. As a result, we frequently end up doing things we don't want to do. As we'll discuss in the next chapter, doing the right thing doesn't always feel good. Self-control involves looking past instant gratification and doing what's right, even when it hurts.

We can get an idea of whether our behavior expresses our love for God by considering the fruits of the Spirit in our lives. How many of them describe you? If someone were writing your obituary, how often would they use the words "love, joy, peace, patience, kindness, goodness, faithfulness, gentleness, self-control"?

Now, don't panic. Asking yourself these questions can be eye-opening and even a little (or very) painful. But we can't fix a lack of fruitfulness unless we first recognize that we have a problem. Once we do that, we can get to work and begin to produce good fruit.

Even though we receive the Holy Spirit in Baptism, he won't force his way into our lives. Nor does the strengthening we receive at Confirmation automatically activate the Spirit. Instead, he waits to be invited. In order to begin the process of producing good fruit, we must give the Holy Spirit permission to go to work. Then we must yield to his promptings and resist the urge to override his power.

If you do these things on a regular basis—invite the Spirit, give him permission, yield to his promptings—you will begin to experience a transformation in your life. Over time you will see more and more evidence of good fruit.

By the way, you can get the ball rolling with three simple words: "Come, Holy Spirit."

Obstacles

We face some unique challenges when we attempt to love God through our behavior. Don't be surprised if some of them look familiar. I have fallen into every one of these booby traps and will probably do so again. Learning to recognize them is half the battle. Learning to overcome them is the other half. Let's explore some obstacles and look at potential solutions.

All in the Mind

When I graduated from college, I decided to start smoking cigarettes. For some reason, it seemed like a good idea at the time. My best friend smoked, smoking helped control my anxiety, and I thought I could quit whenever I wanted to. Unfortunately, it didn't take long for this habit to become an addiction. Eventually, I became concerned about the health risks and thought about quitting.

Rather than actually quitting, however, I repeatedly made the decision to quit "one day" and then lit up another cigarette. I didn't really do anything, but making the decision to quit made me feel better. I went through this cycle many times, never summoning the strength to quit for real. Making the decision to quit smoking at some point in the future fooled me into thinking that I was doing something.

In a similar way, we can make the decision to turn our lives around and start getting serious about God one of these days but still go on living as if he doesn't exist. We may feel good for the moment, but we haven't done anything. That false sense of accomplishment typically happens whenever we read a spiritual book, open the Bible, or hear a great homily and think, "That's a really good message" but do nothing else. St. James was well aware of this problem when he wrote, "But be doers of the word, and not hearers only, deceiving yourselves" (James 1:22).

Typically there will be a time lag between the moment you decide to do something for God and the point when you actually perform the action, but it's good to keep it as short as possible. The longer you wait, the greater the chance that you'll end up doing nothing.

"Why Am I Doing This?"

Because of our fallen human nature, we often end up doing things we regret. Peter, James, and John fell asleep in the Garden of Gethsemane after Jesus asked them to keep him company in his hour of greatest need. Peter failed again when he pledged his loyalty to Jesus and then ended up denying him three times. St. Paul knew all about this stumbling block and wrote about it in his Letter to the Romans: "I do not understand my own actions. For I do not do what I want, but I do the very thing I hate" (7:15).

This obstacle can have devastating consequences, but we can control it through a relatively simple process. Addressing his sleeping followers in the garden, Jesus offered an effective remedy: "Watch and pray that you may not enter into temptation; the spirit indeed is willing, but the flesh is weak" (Matthew 26:41).

Through prayer we can overcome the tendency to seek pleasure above all else. I pray every day for the grace to overcome my spiritual laziness. It's still a temptation, but I'm making progress.

All We Can Do Is Pray!

Does this sound familiar? You're faced with a difficult problem—such as illness, financial difficulty, or family issues—and try everything you can think of to fix it. Nothing works. Someone asks what they can do to help, and you reply, "All we can do is pray."

On the surface, that is an accurate and healthy way to look at the situation. God is infinitely more powerful than we are, and bringing him into the situation is always a good idea. Unfortunately, too often when we use this expression, what we're really doing is downplaying the power of prayer. Basically, we're giving up, not expecting anything, even prayer, to make a difference. Those of us who like to be in control are especially susceptible to falling into this trap.

We may feel better when we are running around doing things, but no human activity is as effective as prayer. As we already established, prayer is not only a behavior but a powerful behavior. Don't let yourself be fooled into thinking that it's a waste of time.

Think back to the story of Martha and Mary. What if Martha had spent some time sitting at the feet of Jesus with Mary, prior to launching into her serving duties? Chances are good that she would have received the grace to work without becoming anxious and troubled.

Don't let prayer be the last thing you do when faced with a crisis. Let it be the first!

> If a brother or sister is poorly clothed and in lack of daily food, and one of you says to them, "Go in peace, be warmed and filled," without giving them the things needed for the body, what does it profit? (James 2:15-16)

Looking Back, Looking Ahead

Thus far we have explored the concept that our love for God is expressed through both our attitude and our behavior. Unless we are working on both, something will be missing. Our decision to love God should lead to some sort of external behavior. We'll delve more into some specific actions in part three, "Serving God," but I wanted to lay some basic groundwork first.

So what's next? In the following chapter, we'll look at how we love God by making a commitment to him. Speaking from experience, I know there are times when we won't feel like praying or doing things for God. Doing it anyway is one of the best ways of showing God how much we love him.

• •

Lord Jesus, I praise and worship you. Thank you for entering our world and redeeming us by your death on the cross. Please lead me into a deeper relationship with the Father, and increase my desire to love him, even when it involves sacrifice. Help me trust you more, and allow me to be transformed by the Holy Spirit into your image. May all of my thoughts, words, and deeds give you glory. Amen.

CHAPTER 6

Keep On Keepin' On!

I have fought the good fight, I have finished the race, I have kept the faith.

—2 Timothy 4:7

I have to be honest and tell you that I've always struggled with commitment. And even though I'd rather not admit it, I have to be even more honest and let you know that one type of commitment has proven especially difficult for me. I've never had difficulty being committed to my marriage, family, or work, but I have struggled with my commitment to God. I have let him down more times than I'd like to acknowledge.

Sound familiar? If so, don't feel bad. It's a common problem. The consequences can be serious (just ask the Israelites, who kept returning to their idols), but we can deal with the issue.

Why is it so difficult to remain committed to God? The most common reason is that we can't see him. He might be all-powerful, but he's also easy to ignore. He respects our free will so much that he will not force us to remain faithful to him.

He will not force me to pray, read the Bible, go to church, or keep the commandments. Other than the gentle nudge of my conscience, God will pretty much remain silent if I choose to ignore him.

Conversely, the distractions of the world are very visible. Constantly bombarded with a flood of in-your-face temptations, we can find it challenging to remain faithful to God.

Nonetheless, we can't truly claim to love God to the best of our ability unless we maintain a decent degree of faithfulness to him. This implies being there for him even when we don't feel like it. There are days when I literally force myself to pray, read Scripture, or write. As luck would have it, today is one of those days.

On the way home from weekday Mass, I mentioned to my wife that I felt like grabbing a book, putting my feet up, and relaxing on the deck. But even though I felt like relaxing, I had a deadline to meet, and I knew that I should spend the day writing about remaining faithful to God. How perfect is that?

I sat down to write this even though I was tired and felt like taking the day off. You'll be the ultimate judge, but I feel the Holy Spirit guiding me as I type these words. It seems to be working out. In fact, I think it's the perfect time to write about remaining committed to God.

In this chapter, we'll look at some individuals who remained faithful to God even when it wasn't easy. We'll also look at some common obstacles to faithfulness and explore ways to overcome them.

Remaining faithful to God isn't overly complicated, but it can be tricky. If we persevere and honor our commitment to him, even when we don't feel like it, we truly demonstrate how much we love him.

Wherever You Go, I Will Go

The Book of Ruth offers one of my favorite examples of commitment. During a time of famine in Israel, a man named Elimelech left his home in Bethlehem and went with his wife, Naomi, and two sons to live in the country of Moab. After the death of Elimelech, Naomi's sons married Moabite women—Ruth and Orpah. Ten years later, the men died, and Naomi was left with no husband and no sons. With no one to provide for her, she was completely helpless.

After hearing that the famine in her homeland was over, Naomi and her daughters-in-law prepared to leave Moab and go to Bethlehem. As they traveled, however, Naomi thanked the women for their kindness and suggested that they return home to their mothers. At first they objected, but eventually Orpah decided to return to her people. Ruth, on the other hand, refused to leave Naomi's side. Her strong commitment to her mother-in-law is evident.

"Do not press me to go back and abandon you!

Wherever you go I will go,
  wherever you lodge I will lodge.
Your people shall be my people
  and your God, my God.
Where you die I will die, and there be buried.

> May the LORD do thus to me, and more, if even death
> separates me from you!" (Ruth 1:16-17, NABRE)

Even though it could not have been easy to leave her homeland, Ruth was determined to stay with Naomi. She valued commitment over comfort. Her love for Naomi drove Ruth to put her mother-in-law's happiness before her own.

Ruth's faithfulness to Naomi proved fruitful in more ways than one. Not only did she meet her future husband, Boaz, in Bethlehem and provide for the needs of Naomi, but Ruth also gave birth to Obed. Obed went on to be the grandfather of King David, from whose line would come the Messiah.

Rebuilding the Wall

After being released from captivity in Babylon, the Jewish exiles returned home and began rebuilding the destroyed Temple. They completed that project, but the walls around the city remained in disrepair for many years, leaving the people unprotected and vulnerable. Eventually, the news of the compromised wall reached Nehemiah, a former resident of Jerusalem who was now the cupbearer for King Artaxerxes of Persia. Eager to help his people, Nehemiah requested permission from the king to return home and lead the rebuilding effort (see Nehemiah 1–6).

Sanballat and Tobiah, two government officials in Jerusalem, were not happy with the arrival of Nehemiah nor with the rebuilding project. Eventually Sanballat's anger escalated, and he began to mock and threaten those working on the wall. Despite the threats, Nehemiah's team moved forward with the project.

When the wall was halfway complete, however, the workers began to lose their momentum. They looked at how much more needed to be done and were overwhelmed, doubting they could complete the work. They became paralyzed with fear when enemies threatened to attack.

In the nick of time, Nehemiah stepped in and took charge. He reminded the workers of the importance of their mission and encouraged them to keep going.

> "Do not be afraid of them. Remember the Lord, who is great and terrible, and fight for your brethren, your sons, your daughters, your wives, and your homes." (Nehemiah 4:14)

Faced with the threats of their enemies and the enormity of the rebuilding task, the workers seemed to forget why they were doing the work in the first place and who was on their side. Nehemiah reminded them of their commitment to their families. He also reminded them that almighty God was on their side and that there was no need to be afraid.

Encouraged, the workers continued. Only fifty-two days after beginning the project, they completed the wall.

Most of us can identify with the experience of the wall builders. They began the project full of enthusiasm and hope but became worn down and discouraged because of the drudgery of the work and the threats of the enemy. Eventually they even forgot about God's protection and assistance.

It happens. Don't be surprised when you encounter similar difficulties once you decide to do something for God. Whether you've made the decision to pray more or do good deeds, at some point you will be tempted to quit. Instead of giving up, try following Nehemiah's example and advice.

Even though the rebuilding project was massive and dangerous, Nehemiah never lost sight of his commitment to God and to the people. That focus sustained him and allowed him to encourage the workers when they ran out of gas. He remained mindful of the fact that God would fight for his people, and he even pitched in to help the workers with the physical labor (see Nehemiah 4:20; 5:16). His wholehearted, committed approach is a great example for us.

They Just Wouldn't Give Up!

Remaining committed to Jesus in today's world can be tricky. Every day, sometimes several times each day, the world reminds us why we should place our trust in everything and everyone *but* Jesus. There never seems to be a shortage of individuals who claim that faith in Jesus is nothing more than wishful thinking or unrealistic optimism.

When faced with a cancer diagnosis or extended unemployment, we might feel as if the naysayers may be right. We start off having faith in God, but it fades with time. The longer our prayers seem to go unanswered, the more likely we are to give up on him. But faith leads to faithfulness.

The Bible offers two examples of women who remained committed to Jesus and refused to give up, even though no one would have blamed them for abandoning him. One of these women suffered from a flow of blood for twelve years (see Mark 5:25-34). According to Mosaic law, this rendered her unclean and meant she had to avoid contact with others. To make matters worse, she had spent all she had on doctors and didn't get any better. In fact, she grew sicker.

Despite the years of suffering, however, this woman never gave up the hope of being healed. Hearing about Jesus, she believed that she could be cured simply by touching his garment. Coming up behind him in a crowd, she touched Jesus from behind and was healed instantly.

What would have happened if she had given up after five, seven, or ten years and no longer sought a healing? We can't say for sure. But we do know that she had faith, as Jesus said when he healed her of her condition: "Daughter, your faith has made you well; go in peace, and be healed of your disease" (Mark 5:34).

Despite the fact that this woman had suffered under many physicians, she remained committed to pursuing a healing from Doctor Jesus. Refusing to give up on Jesus is always a good idea.

The Canaanite woman in the Gospel of Matthew can also teach us a lesson about never losing faith in Jesus (see 15:21-28). As Jesus was ministering in Tyre and Sidon, this desperate woman approached him and cried out, "Have mercy on me, O Lord, Son of David; my daughter is severely possessed by a demon" (15:22).

Hearing this story for the first time, we'd expect Jesus to instantly come to the assistance of the woman and heal her daughter. The story doesn't exactly play out like that. His initial reaction is mind-numbing: "He did not answer her a word" (Matthew 15:23).

As shocking as that is, things go downhill from there. After his disciples pleaded with him to send her away, Jesus stated that he was only sent "to the lost sheep of the house of Israel" (Matthew 15:24). Refusing to give up, the woman knelt before Jesus and begged, "Lord, help me" (15:25).

In one of the most disturbing replies in all the Gospels to someone in need, Jesus seemed not only to deny her request but also to refer to her as a dog. Her response? "Yes, Lord, yet even the dogs eat the crumbs that fall from their masters' table" (Matthew 15:27).

After praising the woman's faith, Jesus told her that he would grant her request. And true to his word, the daughter was healed instantly. Without getting into a lot of detail, we can see that Jesus was testing the Canaanite woman's faith, and she passed with flying colors. Her faith led her to be committed to pursuing her goal.

This is one of the most striking examples of faith and humility anywhere in the Bible. Nothing, and I mean nothing, could make this woman give up on Jesus.

"Come Down!"

Jesus devoted his entire life to doing the will of his Father. Despite many challenges and opportunities to abandon his mission, he never did. Strengthened by the power of the Holy Spirit, Jesus remained faithful to his Father. His life gives us the ultimate example of what it looks like to remain committed to God, no matter what.

Jesus' last opportunity to turn his back on the Father came as he hung on the cross. Bleeding and battered, his life gradually fading from his body, he heard the passersby challenge him to do something that he definitely had the power to do:

> And those who passed by derided him, wagging their heads and saying, "You who would destroy the temple and build it in three days, save yourself! If you are the Son of God, come down from the cross." (Matthew 27:39-40)

The religious leaders chimed in with the hecklers, offering to believe in him if he would come down from the cross:

> So also the chief priests, with the scribes and elders, mocked him, saying, "He saved others; he cannot save himself. He is the King of Israel; let him come down now from the cross, and we will believe in him." (Matthew 27:41-42)

Despite these temptations, Jesus remained committed to the will of his Father. He remained faithful right up to the end of his earthly life. It's challenging, but we are called to the same level of faithfulness to God. Jesus knew how difficult it would be, and that's why he sent his Spirit to help us. With the assistance of the Holy Spirit, it is possible for us to remain committed to God. Let Jesus be your example. You can do it.

Obstacles

As with every obstacle we've looked at, a little awareness will go a long way in helping us overcome the challenge of remaining faithful to God. Let's look at a few of the more common obstacles we will encounter once we make the decision to commit our lives to God.

I have personally grappled with each of these challenges. Sometimes I emerged victorious, and other times I failed miserably. The solutions do work, but they're not foolproof. Between our own shortcomings and the attacks of Satan, we have our work cut out for us.

But don't panic. You might lose a battle here and there, but you can still win the war.

Too Difficult

When Jesus first presented the concept of consuming his flesh and blood to his followers, they didn't exactly welcome the idea. This was a radical and shocking teaching that caused division among the people. Recognizing this, Jesus confronted the problem head-on. He forced his followers to make a choice.

> Many of his disciples, when they heard it, said, "This is a hard saying; who can listen to it?" But Jesus, knowing in himself that his disciples murmured at it, said to them, "Do you take offense at this?" (John 6:60-61)

Because this teaching was so challenging, many of Jesus' disciples rejected it. The same thing happens today, and it's not restricted to the Church's teaching on the Eucharist. Many of today's Catholics struggle to accept the Church's position on abortion, same-sex marriage, contraception, and the all-male priesthood. Some even struggle with the basic concept of forgiving those who offend them.

As a result, the same scenario plays out today that played out when Jesus presented hard truths two thousand years ago: some Christians accept the teachings of Jesus, and some refuse. "After this many of his disciples drew back and no longer walked with him. Jesus said to the Twelve, 'Will you also go away?'" (John 6:66-67).

Each of us must answer that question every day. Commitment to Jesus can be challenging. It can (and will) stretch us and take us out of our comfort zone. We can lose friends and even look foolish. That's the challenge of remaining committed to Christ in a world that emphasizes instant gratification, comfort, and pleasure.

Many Catholics have left the Church, and more will leave because they don't accept certain teachings. It's a serious problem and one that is likely to get worse. Fortunately, we can overcome this obstacle by getting to know Jesus Christ. I've tried this, and it really does work.

Spend time with Jesus in prayer, in Scripture, and in the sacraments. Get to know him as a friend and as a savior. Ask the Holy Spirit to make him real for you. Over time, you'll find yourself more willing to comply with his teachings, even if you don't fully understand them.

Trust me. I've been there.

What Will I Have to Give Up?

It's hardly a secret that Jesus and those who hung out with him weren't exactly wealthy. Furthermore, it can certainly be said that some degree of sacrifice or suffering went along with following him. Heck, Jesus himself said that self-denial and cross carrying were requirements for following him. "And he said to all, 'If any man would come after me, let him deny himself and take up his cross daily and follow me'" (Luke 9:23).

It's easy, therefore, to see why many people are afraid to make the commitment to him. Often the fear of suffering and sacrifice overtakes our desire to follow Jesus. This isn't a new problem. Those who encountered Jesus in the flesh often experienced the same fear. Ultimately they had to make a choice, just as we do.

One day while Jesus was teaching, a young man approached him and asked what he must do to gain eternal life (see Matthew 19:16-22). Jesus instructed him to keep the commandments. The young man pressed for specifics, and Jesus gave him the standard list—you shall not kill, you shall not commit adultery, you shall not steal, you shall not bear false witness, and so on. The man continued to push Jesus: "All these I have observed; what do I still lack?" (19:20). Jesus instructed the young man to sell his possessions, give to the poor, and follow him. The man's response?

"When the young man heard this he went away sorrowful; for he had great possessions" (Matthew 19:22).

> The man was committed to following Jesus but not
> committed enough to give up his wealth.

Each of us will have to deal with this temptation to hold back something from God. It might not be money or possessions that tempt us to abandon our commitment to Jesus. It could be a person or even a desire to be in control. You will have to choose between Jesus and that other thing, just as the young man in the Gospel had to choose.

The best way to overcome this obstacle is to focus on the promise of eternal life. Worldly pleasure is temporary, no matter how appealing it may seem. The eternal happiness promised by Jesus will last forever. You might have to wait to receive your reward, but it will be worth it.

> Therefore, since we are surrounded by so great a cloud
> of witnesses, let us also lay aside every weight, and sin
> which clings so closely, and let us run with persever-
> ance the race that is set before us, looking to Jesus the
> pioneer and perfecter of our faith, who for the joy that
> was set before him endured the cross, despising the
> shame, and is seated at the right hand of the throne of
> God. (Hebrews 12:1-2)

Looking Back, Looking Ahead

Remaining committed to God requires effort on our part. As we have discussed, there will be times when we don't feel like praying, reading the Bible, or doing the right thing. We will encounter circumstances or situations that challenge our faith. Responding with a deliberate act of faith, regardless of how we feel, lets God know just how much we love him. We can choose to remain with him or to abandon him. Many will choose to leave, as the disciples did when Jesus presented the radical notion of eating his flesh and drinking his blood.

You won't hear Jesus speak in an audible manner, as the disciples did when he asked them if they would leave him, but you'll definitely hear him speak through circumstances and temptations. Your circumstances may be challenging, but you have a supernatural advantage at your disposal. Faithfulness is one of the fruits of the Holy Spirit. Make it a point to ask the Holy Spirit every day to help you remain committed to God. It will make a big difference.

Now that we've looked at knowing and loving God, it's time to look at some specific ways to serve him. No matter who you are and where you live, God can and will use you as his instrument. By using your talents and abilities, you can be his hands and feet in the world.

• •

Holy Spirit, I praise and worship you. Thank you for living inside me, just as you lived in Jesus. I give you permission to transform me into his image and to help me do the Father's will. Please inspire my thoughts, words, and deeds so that God can use me to share his kingdom on earth. I ask this in Jesus' name. Amen.

PART THREE

SERVING GOD

Whatever your task, work heartily, as serving the Lord and not men, knowing that from the Lord you will receive the inheritance as your reward; you are serving the Lord Christ.

—Colossians 3:23-24

Once I made up my mind to know God, it didn't take long for me to fall in love with him. As we have seen in previous chapters, however, knowing and loving God don't happen automatically. We have a major part to play. The same principle applies to serving God.

Shortly after I began to know and love God, I began to feel a desire to serve him; this tends to happen as we grow closer to him. If we accept our desire to serve, place ourselves at his disposal, and offer to be his instruments, he will use us. Even better, we have a choice in how, when, and where we will serve.

In this section, we'll take a look at some of the specifics of how we can serve God by caring for his people. We'll focus on three specific aspects of serving God—serving him by serving others, using our God-given talents to do so, and recognizing that God has a specific mission for each of us. Let's take a quick look at each of those now.

Whatsoever You Do . . . At some point, our love for God must manifest itself in loving other people. In fact, that's what serving God is all about. As the First Letter of John so plainly states, "He who does not love his brother whom he has seen, cannot love God whom he has not seen" (4:20). When we serve others, we serve God.

One Body, Many Gifts. No two people receive the same exact gifts from God. St. Paul, in his First Letter to the Corinthians, makes the point that there are many spiritual gifts in the body of Christ—the Church—allowing each member to contribute in a unique way (see chapter 12). By working together and using our complementary gifts, we each play a role in building up God's kingdom on earth.

Bloom Where You're Planted. Nothing about your life is accidental. God chose you to be alive at a certain period in time, within which your life would unfold. The geographical region in which you live, the vocation you choose, your particular family members and friends—all these offer specific ways to serve him. Recognizing and embracing the opportunities offered by your circumstances and choices can make for a productive and fruitful life.

No matter how limited or inadequate you may feel, God wants to use you to build up his kingdom on earth. Nobody is too old, sick, weak, or insignificant to serve God in a big way. You are called to serve God today in a way that is unique to you. How you serve—or whether you serve—will have an impact on the growth of God's kingdom.

There's plenty of work to be done. Ready to get busy?

CHAPTER 7

Whatsoever You Do

Let your light so shine before men, that they may see your good works and give glory to your Father who is in heaven.
—Matthew 5:16

Let's get something out of the way at the beginning of this chapter. It's something I'd rather not admit, but it's 100-percent true.

Sometimes I wish there were a way to serve God without having to serve other people. Wow! That wasn't easy for me to say, but I think it was necessary. Why? Because I know I'm not the only one who feels that way. And we have to admit it if we're truly serious about serving God.

The fact of the matter is, it's much easier to serve an invisible God than to serve visible people, especially when the people are annoying. Jesus knew that this would be challenging for us. That's why, in the Gospel of Matthew, he spoke about the sheep, the goats, and the final judgment (see 25:31-46).

Pointing to the time when he will come in glory, Jesus describes sitting on his throne and gathering the nations before him. He will separate one from another, "as a shepherd separates the sheep from the goats" (Matthew 25:32). He will place the sheep on his right and the goats on the left. Then he will say to those on his right,

> Come, O blessed of my Father, inherit the kingdom prepared for you from the foundation of the world; for I was hungry and you gave me food, I was thirsty and you gave me drink, I was a stranger and you welcomed me, I was naked and you clothed me, I was sick and you visited me, I was in prison and you came to me. (25:34-36)

According to Jesus, the righteous will then ask the obvious question—"When did we see you hungry . . . , sick, or in prison?" Jesus will reply: "Truly, I say to you, as you did it to one of the least of these my brethren, you did it to me" (Matthew 25:37, 39, 40).

God calls us to serve other people—the least among us, first and foremost. When we do that, we serve Jesus. According to him, our salvation depends on it. Now, that's important!

We are also called to serve all those we encounter, a fact we'll also look at in this chapter.

An Unforgettable Lesson

Jesus made it clear that he came to serve, not to be served (see Matthew 20:28). Knowing it was likely that we would conveniently forget his words, he did something designed to make a lasting impression on us.

On the night before he died, Jesus gathered his apostles together for a Passover meal that has come to be known as the Last Supper. After the meal, Jesus rose from the table, took off his outer robe, and wrapped a towel around his waist. Then he took a basin of water, washed the feet of his disciples, and dried them with the towel (see John 13:1-17)

Many of us are so familiar with this story and its reenactment in the Holy Thursday liturgy that we may be unaware of its full significance. Foot washing was a nasty job back in Jesus' day. The wearing of sandals, combined with dusty roads, made for some very dirty feet. The Lord's willingness to embrace such a menial task showed extreme humility.

We may not be shocked by the foot washing, but his disciples sure were. This becomes apparent in the reaction of Simon Peter.

> He came to Simon Peter; and Peter said to him, "Lord, do you wash my feet?" Jesus answered him, "What I am doing you do not know now, but afterward you will understand." Peter said to him, "You shall never wash my feet." (John 13:6-8)

Eventually Peter relented, and Jesus washed his feet. After completing his task, Jesus returned to his seat and plainly stated the point he wanted to make:

> "Do you know what I have done to you? You call me Teacher and Lord; and you are right, for so I am. If I then,

your Lord and Teacher, have washed your feet, you also ought to wash one another's feet. For I have given you an example, that you also should do as I have done to you. Truly, truly, I say to you, a servant is not greater than his master; nor is he who is sent greater than he who sent him." (John 13:12-16)

Jesus wasn't simply illustrating his kindness or proving his humility. This wasn't just a matter of him showing that he was willing to assume the role of a servant. The washing of the apostles' feet was a lesson, an example, and a call to action—not only for those at the Last Supper but also for us.

Where the Rubber Hits the Road

By listening to Jesus and following his example, we get a general idea of what service is all about. Essentially, we are called to serve God by serving those around us. In reality, however, some additional details would help. What does this type of service look like in my daily life? What exactly should I be doing?

The Church helps us out here, offering guidelines that make the concept of serving God by serving others more concrete. These guidelines, known as the works of mercy, list the general needs of humanity—for food, water, consolation, and more. By focusing on these needs, we can devise practical ways to move from the idea of serving God to the reality.

The works of mercy are divided into two categories—corporal and spiritual—because people have both bodily (corporal) and spiritual needs. God wants to use you to help meet the needs of suffering people. Let's look at some ways to do so.

Corporal Works of Mercy

According to the United States Conference of Catholic Bishops (USCCB), the corporal works of mercy can be defined as follows:

> The Corporal Works of Mercy are found in the teachings of Jesus and give us a model for how we should treat all others, as if they were Christ in disguise. They "are charitable actions by which we help our neighbors in their bodily needs" (*United States Catholic Catechism for Adults*). They respond to the basic needs of humanity as we journey together through this life. [2]

Feed the Hungry

According to Catholic Relief Services, roughly eight hundred million people around the world suffer from malnutrition.[3] We can contribute to charitable organizations that help the hungry, and we should. By contributing to these groups, we feed the hungry "Jesuses" around the world.

We don't have to travel far to encounter hunger, however, and we can do more than contribute money. We can join volunteer efforts to feed the hungry locally, in our neighborhood or in our town. Your local church would be a great place to find out more information about how you can help stamp out hunger in your area.

Give Drink to the Thirsty

Many of us can't imagine life without an unlimited supply of clean drinking water, but in many parts of the world, safe water is a luxury. On their Divine Mercy website, the Marian Fathers offer a reflection on the meaning of thirst. They provide sobering statistics from water.org, a nonprofit dedicated to working for clean water globally:

> Nearly 1 billion people lack access to a supply of safe water. More than 3.4 million people a year die from water-related diseases. Every 21 seconds a child in the world dies of such diseases. Nearly one-fifth of all childhood deaths are caused by diarrhea, which kills more young children than AIDS, TB, and malaria combined.[4]

Contributing to Catholic Relief Services and other charitable organizations that work to provide clean water for those in need can be a first step. But again, you might find opportunities on a local level to address the issue of clean water, particularly in impoverished rural areas. For example, in the United States, an estimated two million people lack access to clean water. If you are able, look for ways to take an active role in giving drink to the thirsty in your own town or county.

Shelter the Homeless

You can shelter the homeless in many ways, from financially supporting homeless shelters and similar organizations to volunteering in your parish if, for example, it serves as a warming center for the homeless during cold winter days. You might be able to take in foster children or adopt or join a ministry dedicated to bringing affordable housing to your area. Undoubtedly, you can find volunteer opportunities nearby. And keep this in mind, from the USCCB website:

> There are millions of children and families who are on the move, fleeing from war, illness, hunger and impossible living conditions, and searching for peace and safety. Engage parish groups of children, youth, young adults, and families in doing some research on the causes and challenges that these families face to survive. Contact Catholic Social Services, or diocesan offices of peace and justice for help with your research. Seek ways to provide shelter for the homeless locally, regionally, nationally or internationally.[5]

Visit the Sick

You don't have to look hard to find sick people to visit—sometimes they even live with you. A parent sitting by the bedside of a sick child or a wife tending to the needs of her dementia-stricken husband are practical examples of this work of mercy.

Ministering to the sick is best done in person, but you can also do it over the phone, by mail, and through face-to-face calls over your computer or phone. Even if you can't do any of these things, it's possible to "visit" the sick by saying a prayer.

Visit Prisoners

Don't feel bad if you're not comfortable venturing inside the walls of a prison. It's a special calling and definitely not for everyone. That doesn't mean that you can't reach out to bring God's love to inmates. Many churches and ministries offer pen pal opportunities, allowing volunteers to correspond anonymously with prisoners. And you might also ask locally if there are other volunteer opportunities, such as gathering books for the prison library or tutoring a prisoner over the internet.

Finally, don't forget that not all prisoners are found behind bars. Some are disabled and imprisoned in their own homes or in nursing homes. Others are held captive by anxiety or mental illness. Your visit, either in person or in some other way, can allow them to feel God's presence and love.

Bury the Dead

Death is inevitable, but we often go to great lengths to avoid thinking about it. As a result, we can ignore the opportunity a funeral provides to prayerfully commend a deceased loved one to the Lord.

Arranging a proper Christian funeral is a great work of mercy on behalf of the dead. And whenever we participate in a funeral liturgy for a friend or family member, we perform a work of mercy. We also do this by praying for the deceased and having Masses offered for them.

Give Alms to the Poor

Have you ever wondered why a loving God allows some people to live in extreme poverty? It's a reasonable question. Instead of blaming God for this, I recommend that we view it as an opportunity to be used as his instruments.

We can and should pray for those who are impoverished, but we can often do more. By sharing some of what we have with those in need, we can help end poverty. Looking at it from this point of view helps us see that God really is helping those in need. He's doing it through us.

Spiritual Works of Mercy

In addition to providing for the bodily needs of those around us, God also expects us to provide for their spiritual needs. According to the USCCB,

> The Spiritual Works of Mercy have long been a part of the Christian tradition, appearing in the works of theologians and spiritual writers throughout history. Just as Jesus attended to the spiritual well-being of those he ministered to, these Spiritual Works of Mercy guide us to "help our neighbor in their spiritual needs."[6]

Let's take a brief look at each of the spiritual works of mercy.

Counsel the Doubtful

At some point, we all experience doubt as part of our journey with God. An unanswered prayer, a sudden death—any number of situations can stir up doubt. It will happen. The silver lining here is that struggling with our own questions can prepare us to help others who struggle. It might be difficult to hear a loved one question the existence of God or wonder why God is letting them suffer, but these occasions allow us to serve God by encouraging his people.

A few years ago, I found myself struggling to trust in God's providence. I called my good friend Jeff, who was able to restore my confidence in God with two simple words—"Just trust." Sometimes that's all it takes.

Instruct the Ignorant

Don't be distracted by the use of the word "ignorant." It may sound harsh, but in this case, it simply refers to a lack of knowledge about the faith.

There may be someone in your workplace who doesn't know that God loves them or doesn't understand that Jesus is fully present in the Eucharist. A fellow parishioner may not be aware of the Lord's power to heal even serious illness. Your spouse or child may be carrying a heavy burden from past sins, unaware of God's desire to forgive them.

Tell them the good news. Share the Church's teaching with them. That's how we instruct the ignorant.

Admonish the Sinner

This is a tricky one. We have a responsibility to speak to others, primarily fellow Christians, about their behavior when it is seriously immoral, but we should exercise a great deal of caution when doing so. Before we attempt to address someone's problematic behavior, we should consider our motive. We must be motivated by love, not by the need to show them we're right. It's not always easy to tell the difference.

Ask the Holy Spirit to guide you. If you decide to move forward, pray that you know the proper time and place. You never want to correct someone in public—or on social media, which is a huge trap—or at the wrong time.

When it comes to admonishing the sinner, rely heavily on the help of the Holy Spirit, and don't force the matter. And remember St. Paul's advice: always correct others "in a spirit of gentleness" (Galatians 6:1).

Comfort the Sorrowful

Many people find wakes and funerals extremely stressful. For one thing, people often feel that they don't know what to say. I hated to go to viewings for that very reason, until my wife shared something that completely changed my outlook.

When Eileen was nineteen, her father died suddenly. Many people attended the viewing, and this was a great comfort to her. She told me, "You don't even remember what people say. You just feel good that they're there."

Don't worry about finding the right words. Your presence is what matters most.

Forgive Injuries

It is essential that we forgive those who offend us. When it comes to the question of just how essential, I'll defer to the words of Jesus. He said it better than I ever could.

> "For if you forgive men their trespasses, your heavenly Father also will forgive you; but if you do not forgive men their trespasses, neither will your Father forgive your trespasses." (Matthew 6:14-15)

Jesus didn't say we have to feel it; he said we have to do it. Choosing to forgive those who offend us is a conscious decision, not a feeling.

Bear Wrongs Patiently

Closely related to forgiving those who offend us, this work of mercy embraces forgiveness as an ongoing process. Throughout his public ministry, Jesus patiently endured a constant barrage of hatred and persecution. With the help of the Holy Spirit, we can learn to do the same.

Some degree of persecution goes along with living an authentic Christian life. But exercising this spiritual work of mercy does not mean subjecting yourself to abusive or dangerous relationships. If someone abuses you physically or verbally, the Church doesn't expect you to remain in the line of fire. You can and should do what you can to escape the situation.

Pray for the Living and the Dead

It's a great privilege to pray for others, especially knowing that God hears and answers our prayers. We don't have to understand how prayer works to know that it *is* working, even if the answers seem to be something other than what we asked for. Whether we understand or not, we just have to do it!

Praying for the dead is a special privilege: we know they depend on our prayers as they move into their new life, beyond time and space. This intercessory prayer is a mystery but also a responsibility. We must take seriously the call to pray for those who have gone before us.

Obstacles

The best way to serve God is by serving other people. Sounds simple, doesn't it? But we know it's not easy to put into practice.

The obstacles to serving God are many, but there are a few themes common to most of them. Let's examine a couple of these challenges and explore ways to overcome them.

People Can Be Annoying

I could probably find a more delicate way to state this, but I don't think it would be as effective. People can be so annoying; am I right? We have all encountered individuals who drive us crazy.

It's so much easier to serve an invisible God than it is to serve the miserable person who never seems to appreciate anything we do for them. Nonetheless, the fact remains that if we truly want to serve God, we will have to find a way to look past the annoying qualities of those around us and serve them. Gritting your teeth and forcing yourself to serve them will only get you so far. Eventually, you'll run out of gas and give up.

What has worked for me is a combination of prayer and cooperation with the grace that flows from my prayer. In order to maintain a sustained desire to serve others, we need to see others as Jesus sees them. If we ask, God will give us the grace to make this happen.

With the help of the Holy Spirit, we can also begin to identify one or two good qualities in those people we find difficult. Be forewarned that this is not easy to do; you will be tempted to stop praying in this way. But I strongly recommend you persevere. It is definitely worth it.

What's in It for Me?

Like it or not, we have a fallen human nature. This tends to make us selfish, and we desire comfort. In order to serve others, we must put their happiness ahead of our own. As with other obstacles in this book, the first step is to recognize the problem and accept that it exists.

Once again, grace is a valuable aid to overcoming our human weaknesses. Every day I ask the Holy Spirit to inspire my thoughts, words, and deeds and to transform me into the image of Jesus. That's his job, and he does it well.

Unfortunately for those of us who struggle with patience, this transformation takes time. It's a process. Nonetheless, it does work. I don't see a change every day, but I see that I'm less selfish than I was a year ago.

If you ask God to increase your desire to help others, he will respond. The key is to keep asking. Don't allow yourself to become discouraged. Your prayer will bear fruit.

> For you were called to freedom, brethren; only do not use your freedom as an opportunity for the flesh, but through love be servants of one another. (Galatians 5:13)

Looking Back, Looking Ahead

In this chapter, we've discussed some concrete, practical ways to serve God by serving those around us. The opportunities exist; we need to recognize and embrace them.

Now it's time to get more specific about the fact that the Lord has given each of us unique gifts. In the following chapter, we'll examine some of these talents and discuss ways to use them in the service of God.

• •

Holy Spirit, I turn to you today and ask you to transform me so that I think, speak, and act like Jesus and am ever mindful of doing the will of the Father. Grant me the grace to see the goodness in those around me. Help me overcome my selfish desires and seek to serve others.

I ask this with confidence, knowing that you will hear and answer me. Amen.

CHAPTER 8

One Body, Many Gifts

As each has received a gift, employ it for one another, as good stewards of God's varied grace.

—1 Peter 4:10

In December of 2017, I left my full-time speaking and writing ministry to work as the director of parish services at Mary, Mother of the Redeemer Parish in North Wales, Pennsylvania. It was a difficult decision, but after much prayer, I felt that this was where the Lord wanted me to be.

This job required me to move out of my comfort zone. Although I had been involved in parish ministry as a volunteer for many years, I had never been officially employed in a parish. I remained in the job for fifteen months, and the experience proved to be both challenging and eye-opening. I learned a great deal from it.

So what is a director of parish services anyway? Essentially, my duties involved adult faith formation and event planning. The first part came easy. I was responsible for helping parishioners draw closer to God, something I was doing anyway but now would be doing in a formal way. I always enjoyed that aspect of my job and had freedom in the parish to do it as I saw fit.

On the other hand, the event planning part of the position was extremely challenging. Much to his credit, Msgr. John Conway, the pastor, recognized that I had no experience in running events and was very patient with me. When he offered me the position, he emphasized that I didn't have to do everything by myself. He encouraged me to seek help from parishioners, many of whom were anxious to pitch in. That proved to be excellent advice.

So how did my strengths and weaknesses play out as I served the parish? God has gifted me with the ability to do some things well, just as he has gifted you. It doesn't take extraordinary effort to do these things; they come naturally. Furthermore, performing these tasks doesn't cause a great deal of stress. For example, I have no problem writing and speaking about Jesus, I'm comfortable doing radio and TV interviews, and I really enjoy leading Bible studies.

On the other hand, the thought of organizing a senior luncheon or a women's retreat was enough to cause me to break out in a cold sweat. Actually, my all-time most dreaded event was the annual Advent wreath-making extravaganza. I still cringe when I think about it.

Here's what I learned during my time at the parish: my weaknesses are someone else's strengths. Bobbi was great at ordering food and running luncheons, Melanie and Chris developed a brilliant concept for a senior adult ministry (SAM!), Valerie and several others used their creative abilities to ensure that the Advent wreath-making event wasn't a total disaster. And then there were Barb and Kathy, who did a little bit of everything, including functioning as my spiritual "bodyguards."

Without the help of these and many other individuals, I would not have been able to carry out the duties of my job or adequately serve the parishioners. When we all pitched in and used our God-given gifts, everything came together perfectly.

Different Ways to Serve

So what do you do with the unique talents God has given you? Yes, you heard that correctly. God himself has given you an individualized combination of skills that you can use to serve him by serving his people.

Writing to the church in Corinth, St. Paul observed:

> Now there are varieties of gifts, but the same Spirit; and there are varieties of service, but the same Lord; and there are varieties of working, but it is the same God who inspires them all in every one. To each is given the manifestation of the Spirit for the common good. (1 Corinthians 12:4-7)

He goes on to list some of the gifts that flow from the power of the Holy Spirit, including some unusual ones:

> To one is given through the Spirit the utterance of wisdom, and to another the utterance of knowledge according to the same Spirit, to another faith by the same

> Spirit, to another gifts of healing by the one Spirit, to another the working of miracles, to another prophecy, to another the ability to distinguish between spirits, to another various kinds of tongues, to another the interpretation of tongues. (1 Corinthians 12:8-10)

Sometimes referred to as charismatic gifts, these manifestations of the Spirit, or charisms, are given to individuals in order to build up the body of Christ on earth. Anyone involved in the Catholic Charismatic Renewal will be familiar with the gifts of healing, speaking in tongues, and prophecy. The *Catechism* acknowledges their existence and usefulness:

> Whether extraordinary or simple and humble, charisms are graces of the Holy Spirit which directly or indirectly benefit the Church, ordered as they are to her building up, to the good of men, and to the needs of the world. (799)

Now, here's where we have to be careful. When we look at St. Paul's list of extraordinary charisms, we can think of the gifts of the Holy Spirit in a narrow manner. In his Letter to the Romans, Paul describes some additional ways in which the Holy Spirit can work through the members of the Church. Some of these gifts are so ordinary that we might overlook the fact that they are indeed spiritual gifts.

> For as in one body we have many members, and all the members do not have the same function, so we, though many, are one body in Christ, and individually members

one of another. Having gifts that differ according to the grace given to us, let us use them: if prophecy, in proportion to our faith; if service, in our serving; he who teaches, in his teaching; he who exhorts, in his exhortation; he who contributes, in liberality; he who gives aid, with zeal; he who does acts of mercy, with cheerfulness. (Romans 12:4-8)

You may not consider serving, teaching, contributing, giving aid, and performing acts of mercy to be gifts of the Holy Spirit, but they are. By using these gifts, we can all play a part in serving God and building up his kingdom on earth. Once again turning to the writings of St. Paul, consider his words to the church at Ephesus:

And his gifts were that some should be apostles, some prophets, some evangelists, some pastors and teachers, to equip the saints for the work of ministry, for building up the body of Christ. (Ephesians 4:11-12)

The Church benefits whenever we use our unique gifts to serve those around us. It might not seem like a big deal to you, but it really is a big deal to God. Any act of service we perform, no matter how small, can have a ripple effect and be pleasing to God.

Think Your Job Isn't Important? Think Again!

Sometimes we think that in order to serve God, we have to do it in a big way. As a result, we wait for the huge project to come our way so that we can step into action. In the meantime, many ordinary opportunities for service come and go. Don't fall into this trap.

We have many chances to serve God every day. Those apparently unimportant tasks that are so easy to overlook give us the chance to be part of God's miracles. Think I'm kidding? Here are a few examples from the Bible.

Five Loaves and Two Fish

After a long day of preaching to a crowd of five thousand men along with women and children—possibly as many as ten thousand people—Jesus and his apostles faced a serious predicament: how to feed the hungry multitude. Thinking in purely human terms, the apostles suggested that Jesus send the crowd away so that the people could buy food. Turning the tables, Jesus instructed his apostles to feed the people themselves.

Andrew, the brother of Simon Peter, tried to make sense of the Lord's instructions. He responded in a way that reflected both obedience and practicality: "There is a lad here who has five barley loaves and two fish; but what are they among so many?" (John 6:9).

You probably know what happened next. Jesus asked for the five loaves and two fish, and he went on to perform a miracle so important that all four Gospels include it (see Matthew 14:13-21; Mark 6:32-44; Luke 9:10-17; John 6:1-13). Furthermore, Jesus used the "trivial" act of the young boy handing over his lunch as part of a powerful miracle.

Fill 'Em Up!

Jesus performed his first recorded miracle at a wedding at Cana in Galilee (see John 2:1-11). This story is often used as an illustration of Mary's intercessory power. While her role justifiably gets most of the attention, we shouldn't overlook the part played by the servants. After Mary instructs them, "Do whatever he tells you" (2:5), they perform two seemingly ordinary tasks that end up being an important part of the Lord's miracle:

> Jesus said to them, "Fill the jars with water." And they filled them up to the brim. He said to them, "Now draw some out, and take it to the steward of the feast." So they took it. (2:7-8)

What would have happened if the servants had refused to fill up the jars with water or had rejected Jesus' instructions to take the water, now transformed into wine, to the steward? We don't know what would have happened if they refused, but the Bible clearly tells us what *did* happen when they obeyed. Their actions became an important part of a miracle that manifested the glory of Jesus (see John 2:11) and led his disciples to believe in him. Those ordinary tasks the servants performed don't look so ordinary now, do they?

If at First You Don't Succeed . . .

A fisherman by trade, Simon Peter knew how to fish. Even if, by some chance, he wasn't good at what he did, it's safe to say that he knew more about catching fish than someone who didn't fish for a living. With that in mind, let's take a look at what happened when Jesus showed up at Peter's workplace and they interacted for the first time.

> Getting into one of the boats, which was Simon's, he asked him to put out a little from the land. And he sat down and taught the people from the boat. And when he had ceased speaking, he said to Simon, "Put out into the deep and let down your nets for a catch." And Simon answered, "Master, we toiled all night and took nothing! But at your word I will let down the nets." And when they had done this, they enclosed a great shoal of fish; and as their nets were breaking, they beckoned to their partners in the other boat to come and help them. And they came and filled both the boats, so that they began to sink. (Luke 5:3-7)

There was something about this carpenter that led Peter to take advice from him. Though tired and frustrated from working all night and catching nothing, Peter chose to listen to Jesus and do what he had already spent the night doing. He let down the nets and, as a result of this simple and ordinary action, caught enough fish to fill the nets and two boats!

This development so affected Peter, Andrew, James, and John that they left everything to become apostles of Jesus. And it all started with the routine task of lowering a fishing net. Wow!

Getting Personal

So where do we go from here?

Recognizing the fact that there are many ways to serve God and acknowledging that we can serve him in ordinary ways are a good start, but it's not enough. At some point, we need to get busy and actually start serving him. If you've been doing this, great job!

If you're not sure where to begin or if you're interested in exploring new ways to serve God, I'd like to share something I learned over the years. Serving God begins by answering two simple questions: *What am I good at?* and *What needs to be done?*

What Am I Good At?

Supernatural talents, or gifts, often flow out of our natural abilities and interests. If you're good at working with children, you might be a good religious education teacher. Are you musical? Parishes are constantly in need of singers and musicians. Your math skills may come in handy with counting the Sunday collections or handling financial transactions at parish fundraisers. Are you comfortable with public speaking? Chances are that you would make a good lector at Mass.

Over the years, I have played guitar in the music ministry, produced a newsletter for a church group, distributed Holy Communion at a nursing home, led an adult faith-sharing small group, and collected donations outside stores for the Knights of Columbus. For the most part, all these tasks were based on my natural gifts, and doing the work came easily for me.

Most of us have a general idea of our strengths and weaknesses. I know mine. Because of this, I have never attempted to teach young children, lead the singing at church, or do anything involving math.

What Needs to Be Done?

We have established that the best way to serve God is to serve others. But how?

One of the best ways to start is to look for opportunities. Your parish probably offers some good ones, but you should also consider the needs of your family, friends, and community. Look around and see who needs help.

Don't think that serving God must be done in a formal way. Maybe your elderly neighbor needs a ride to the store or someone to talk to. Is there a relative or friend who could use a phone call or text? Maybe your spouse, child, or parent needs a hand. All of these offer opportunities to serve God.

Before we move on to obstacles, I want to address one more thing. Sometimes God will plant the desire in you to do something that you've never done before. You may not understand why you have the desire to serve him in a certain way, but you do. Here's an example.

I have always been a shy person, and I had no experience, early on, as a writer, public speaker, or radio broadcaster. All my work experience was in the software industry. After my conversion, when I surrendered my life to Christ, I gradually felt called to proclaim the good news in a public way. It started with a desire to be a lector at Mass and progressed from there. It didn't make sense for me to feel this way, but the desire didn't go away.

If you feel that God is calling you to do something out of your comfort zone, don't ignore it. Pray about it, get sound spiritual advice—I had a great spiritual director—take your time, and wait for God to open the right doors. He will lead you to where you're supposed to be.

Obstacles

As you might expect, there are many reasons why we fail to use our talents in serving God and his people. Before we look at a few of the more common obstacles, I want to emphasize that every one of us has some gift that can be used to serve God. Sometimes a little digging is necessary to uncover it, but it's there.

Keeping that in mind, let's explore a few of the obstacles you may encounter in discovering and using your gifts. And of course, we'll look at ways to overcome them.

The Exception to the Rule

Have you ever felt that God somehow overlooked you when he was handing out talents? Don't panic. Most of us have felt that way at one point or another.

Just because we feel it, however, doesn't make it true. If you have the desire to serve God, he can and will use you. Satan will often try to convince you that you lack what it takes, but he is a liar. Don't believe him!

If you've made the decision to serve God but don't know where to start, I recommend that you pray about it. Simply tell God that you wish to be used as his instrument, and ask him to guide you. This is a good prayer to use at the start of your day.

Praying in this manner is important even if you're already involved in some form of ministry or service. God will often use us in unexpected ways and places—the grocery store, doctor's office, gas station, for example—when we remain open to the idea of serving him in any way he desires. Boxing him in is always a mistake. There are plenty of opportunities to serve him in the world.

It's Too Difficult

I'm just going to come right out and say this: serving God can be difficult. We touched on the main reason for this in the last chapter: people can be annoying. If we're going to serve God, however, we have to find a way to get beyond this obstacle. Jesus never avoided difficult people, and neither should we.

The first step is to recognize the situation for what it is. People have unique personalities, and interacting with them isn't always pleasant. Keep in mind the fact that when you serve others, you are serving God. Pray for the grace to look beyond the outward appearance and see souls created in the image and likeness of God. It's not always easy, but that's why prayer is so important.

When I worked at the parish, I came in contact with a wide range of personalities. Some of these individuals were very forceful and even abrasive, but I knew God wanted me to serve them. Prayer was a big weapon in my arsenal. It's amazing what can happen when you pray for the grace to see others as God sees them.

But It's So Ordinary

One of the greatest challenges we face when serving God is accepting the fact that what we're doing really matters. We've touched on this previously, but it bears repeating. It doesn't matter if we're sweeping the floor, cleaning the bathroom, serving coffee and donuts after Mass, leading a Bible study, or visiting a sick friend. Any work we do for God is important.

We should want to do something that makes a difference, of course, but that doesn't mean it has to be extraordinary. When in doubt, remember that Jesus spent the first thirty years of his life in relative obscurity. Living an ordinary life with Mary and Joseph, Jesus obeyed the will of his Father by performing the routine duties of his daily life. Use him as your role model.

It doesn't matter what kind of work you're doing. If you're doing it for God, it's important.

> We are to grow up in every way into him who is the head, into Christ, from whom the whole body, joined and knit together by every joint with which it is supplied, when each part is working properly, makes bodily growth and upbuilds itself in love. (Ephesians 4:15-16)

Looking Back, Looking Ahead

There are many different ways to serve God, but it all starts with wanting to serve him. Once that's in place, we can take advantage of our natural skills, because the ability to perform a certain task well often indicates a path forward.

Many years ago, when I was trying to discern how to serve God, I tried to be open to a religious vocation. Someone told me, "If God wants you to be a priest, he'll give you the desire to be a priest." He did give me a desire to serve but not in a religious vocation, and ultimately, I used my natural abilities in other ways on behalf of his kingdom.

Looking ahead to the next chapter, we'll consider the importance of serving him right where we are. God sometimes calls us to move into a new career or relocate to another part of the country or world, but changes of that nature typically take time to come about. For now, we'll discover many opportunities to serve him right where we are, today. Let's get busy!

• •

Jesus, thank you for giving me a unique set of talents and abilities. Open my eyes to see the ways you would like me to serve you. Please open doors and send people into my life who will help me share in your work of advancing God's kingdom on earth. Help me keep my heart set on doing the will of the Father through the promptings of the Holy Spirit. Amen.

CHAPTER 9

Bloom Where You're Planted

"You shall not see your brother's ox or his sheep go astray, and withhold your help from them; you shall take them back to your brother."

—Deuteronomy 22:1

In this chapter, we'll take a look at some examples of serving God in the midst of ordinary and less than ideal circumstances. I chose each of these accounts to help you recognize opportunities to serve God in your own surroundings, especially opportunities that are disguised and easy to overlook. No matter where you are or what is happening in your life, you have the chance to serve God in some way today.

I learned this lesson in a big way when I became involved with a Catholic young adult group in 1992. Organized primarily as a multiparish Catholic spiritual group, Twenty Something or Thereabouts (TSOTA) provided an opportunity for young adults to come together, pray the Rosary, listen to speakers, and socialize. It came at the perfect time for me, since I was very lonely. I had just moved from Pennsylvania to New Jersey and was living on my own for the first time. TSOTA was based in my parish. It seemed to fall into my lap just when I needed it.

I'd like to tell you that I joined the group for spiritual enrichment and to grow closer to the Lord. As a lukewarm Mass-going Catholic, however, I had an ulterior motive. In all honesty, I hoped to meet a nice Catholic woman to marry. The spiritual aspect of the group didn't scare me—I longed for a deeper relationship with God—but it wasn't my main focus. God had a plan, however, as he always does.

After several months of not connecting with a potential spouse, I was frustrated and on the verge of quitting. Before I did, however, I spoke to one of the group's founders, a young woman named Juliana. Although I felt uncomfortable telling her the truth, I came clean and revealed my true motive. Much to my surprise, Juliana laughed and told me that I wasn't alone. To a certain extent, most of the members of the group were there for the same reason.

Juliana also made what turned out to be a life-changing request. "Until you meet your future wife," she asked, "would you consider helping out in some way? We could use a lot of help." Her suggestion stopped me in my tracks. I wasn't exactly thrilled with the idea.

Over the next few months, I went on to provide music for the services, assist with setup and cleanup, write articles for the newsletter, and take care of various other duties. My circumstances didn't feel ideal, but I was finding ways to serve God. It was quite a change for me, and it felt good. Ultimately,

I did meet my wife, Eileen, at the group, but not before I had learned a valuable lesson about what it means to serve God in the present moment.

We can wait until everything falls into place perfectly, or we can get busy and look for ways to serve God today. One way puts our needs first, and the other way puts his needs first. If we are truly looking to serve God, there's no doubt about which option we should choose.

God Has a Plan

Joseph had plenty of reasons to become discouraged with the way life was treating him. His brothers, jealous that their father loved him best, sold him to a group of Ishmaelite traders, who then took him to Egypt and sold him to Potiphar, an officer for Pharaoh (see Genesis 37). Joseph's run of bad luck didn't end there. When he turned down the advances of Potiphar's wife, she falsely accused him of rape. This landed him in prison, where he remained for several years (see chapter 39).

Refusing to give up, Joseph made the most of the opportunity. Pharaoh had a dream that none of his sages could interpret for him. Joseph didn't understand the dream, but he relied on God, telling Pharaoh that God would make the meaning clear. Joseph successfully provided the interpretation, explaining that the dream meant seven years of prosperity for Egypt, followed by seven years of famine. Impressed, Pharaoh rewarded Joseph by placing him in charge of the entire country (see Genesis 41:1-43).

Under Joseph's leadership, the Egyptians stored grain during the seven years of Egyptian prosperity. Then, when famine struck, as Joseph had predicted, they opened the storehouses and distributed the grain to the people. The famine was widespread, and people from around the world came to Egypt to buy grain. When Joseph's father, Jacob, heard that grain was available in Egypt, he sent his sons to obtain some.

When the ten brothers arrived, guess whom they had to see in order to purchase the grain? You guessed it. Their younger brother, Joseph, the one they had sold into slavery. A bit of drama ensued, but the brothers ultimately received the grain they needed, and Jacob, before he died, got to see his son.

The Book of Genesis closes with Joseph forgiving his brothers, in words that display a profound understanding of God's providence:

> As for you, you meant evil against me; but God meant it for good, to bring it about that many people should be kept alive, as they are today. So do not fear; I will provide for you and your little ones. (50:20-21)

Joseph didn't grumble about all the bad breaks that came his way. Instead, he focused on what needed to be done around him. He served God right where he was, in the midst of unpleasant circumstances. As a result, many people survived the famine, including his father and brothers.

Making the Best of a Bad Situation

It wasn't a good time for the residents of Judah. The Babylonians had not only conquered them but had also taken many of them into captivity in Babylon, at the order of King Nebuchadnezzar. The prophet Jeremiah was allowed to remain in Jerusalem, and from there he wrote a letter to the elders, priests, prophets, and all the exiles.

In the letter, Jeremiah relayed a message the Lord had given him. He told the captives that they would be freed but not for another seventy years. It might not have been what they wanted to hear, but it was what they needed to hear.

> Thus says the LORD of hosts, the God of Israel, to all the exiles whom I have sent into exile from Jerusalem to Babylon: Build houses and live in them; plant gardens and eat their produce. Take wives and have sons and daughters; take wives for your sons, and give your daughters in marriage, that they may bear sons and daughters; multiply there, and do not decrease. But seek the welfare of the city where I have sent you into exile, and pray to the LORD on its behalf, for in its welfare you will find your welfare. (Jeremiah 29:4-7)

Even though the exiles were somewhere they didn't want to be, God told them through Jeremiah to get on with their lives and pray for their pagan captors. Instead of sitting around waiting for their circumstances to improve, God wanted them to get to work. It was a call to action. Eventually they'd return to their homeland, but not until they finished their work in Babylon.

For Such a Time as This

The story of Queen Esther is an amazing example of someone being in the right place at the right time. After the Persians conquered Babylon, King Cyrus gave the Jewish exiles permission to return to Jerusalem. Some of them, however, chose to remain in Persia. Although the Jews were a minority and considered foreigners, they had great freedom and plenty of opportunity to establish themselves.

Under the reign of King Ahasuerus, however, things began to change. The chain of events he set in motion ultimately threatened the existence of the Jewish people. God used the circumstances to display his providential love.

King Ahasuerus banished his wife, Queen Vashti, for refusing to obey one of his orders, and he chose a young woman named Esther to be the new queen. He was completely unaware of her Jewish heritage; Esther's cousin, Mordecai, who had adopted her on the death of her parents, advised her to keep that information to herself. Mordecai, a Jewish exile, became a government official after helping foil an assassination plot against the king.

Things looked good for the Jewish residents of Persia, but they began to go downhill when the king appointed a man named Haman to a position of high honor. The king ordered all royal officials to kneel down and pay homage to Haman. Unwilling to bow down to anyone but God, Mordecai refused. Haman, outraged, vowed revenge, not just on Mordecai, but on the entire Jewish population.

Haman convinced King Ahasuerus to sign an order "to destroy, to slay, and to annihilate all Jews, young and old, women and children, in one day" (Esther 3:13). On hearing the news, Mordecai went out into the city dressed in sackcloth and ashes, wailing and crying for his people. He sent word to Queen Esther, asking her to intervene in the matter. She sent back a message reminding him that approaching the king without an invitation could result in her execution. Mordecai in turn reminded her that God had placed her in the middle of this situation for a reason:

> "For if you keep silence at such a time as this, relief and deliverance will rise for the Jews from another quarter, but you and your father's house will perish. And who knows whether you have not come to the kingdom for such a time as this?" (Esther 4:14)

The very existence of the Jewish population depended on Esther's intervention. She was the only one who could get the job done, but she was blinded by fear. Mordecai reminded her that if she didn't save the people, nobody would. She was made "for such a time as this." With Mordecai's encouragement and after much prayer, Esther rose to the occasion. Ultimately, the king condemned Haman to death, and the Jewish population survived.

God's fingerprints are all over this story. He created Esther at a particular point in history and placed her in a position to be his instrument. When she hesitated, God sent Mordecai to remind her of what was at stake. Queen Esther made the best of her circumstances, and God used her in a powerful way—all because she recognized that there was work to be done right where she was.

Obstacles

Serving God where he has placed us—in the midst of the ordinary activities of our lives, no matter how our lives are unfolding—is critical. Any obstacle that causes us to lose sight of concrete, or real, opportunities to serve God in the present moment can hold us back. Let's consider some of these obstacles.

Another Time, Another Place

I used to feel that I was born at the wrong time. Somewhere in my teenage years, I discovered the joy of vintage movies, TV shows, music, comic books, and baseball cards. I'm not sure what the attraction was, but I think it had to do with being transported back to a simpler time. Life in the forties and fifties just seemed less complicated.

As I grew older, my attraction to things of the past grew stronger. I felt I would have fit in better if I had been born a few decades earlier.

At the beginning of this chapter, I told you about my conversation with Juliana (from the twenty-something group), but there's more to the story. While I was chatting with her, I told her about this feeling that I was born at the wrong time. She immediately countered my argument by telling me something I needed to hear.

"You were born at exactly the right time, and so was I," she said. "God willed that we should be alive at this point in history, and he has work for us to do." I've never forgotten that valuable lesson. Her words completely changed my outlook.

Yearning for the past or wishing we were born in a different generation can get in the way of doing the work that God wants us to do. The escapism provided by nostalgia can be attractive, but we have to be careful. God doesn't make mistakes, and he doesn't leave things to chance. It's not an accident that you were born at a certain time.

God chose you to enter the world at the exact point in history when you could do the most good, just as he chose Joseph, the exiles, and Esther for their times. He has surrounded you with specific opportunities to serve him, in the present moment. Don't allow yourself to be so distracted by the past that you fail to see the work God sets before you today.

Nothing to Do Here

How many times have you looked at what's going on in the world and shaken your head in disbelief? That's a reasonable reaction. Every time I go on social media or watch the news, somebody is doing something crazy.

It's not a stretch to say that we live in a crazy world, but we have to be careful where we go with that thought. It's easy to get so caught up in what's going wrong that we overlook our ability to make a difference. The immorality, hatred, and division in the world should make us angry, but that anger should motivate us to take action in a positive, upbuilding manner. You can't fix everything that's broken in the world, but you can do your part to mend and heal. Your actions influence the people around you.

If you choose to serve God today, where he placed you, you will change the world for the better. You really can make a difference. The key is to focus on doing what you can in the circumstances in which you find yourself.

> But I will stay in Ephesus until Pentecost, for a wide door for effective work has opened to me, and there are many adversaries. (1 Corinthians 16:8-9)

Looking Back, Looking Ahead

Throughout this chapter, we have looked at various individuals who made the decision to serve God in the present moment. Instead of lashing out and cursing their circumstances, they sought opportunities to serve. By making the best of a bad situation, they did what God wanted them to do.

As we bring this chapter (and book) to a close, I encourage you to remember that God has placed you where you are for a reason. He created you to perform a specific task that only you can do, serving others in the present moment right where you are. Your task might not seem glamorous or important in your eyes, but God sees it differently. Not only is your work important to him, but it's also what he wants you to do.

And doing that, my friend, is how you get to heaven.

. . . .

Heavenly Father, thank you for allowing me to be born at this time in history. I know that you have work for me to do, and it's an honor to serve you. Please open my eyes so that I can see and perform what needs to be done.

I ask this in Jesus' name and through the power of the Holy Spirit. Amen.

Conclusion

As we have discussed throughout this book, the process of knowing, loving, and serving God can best be described as a journey. Specifically, we refer to it as the journey of faith or our journey with God. As with any journey, there is a clearly defined beginning and end.

Our journey with God begins on the day we are baptized and concludes on the day we die. At that point, faith will no longer be possible or necessary. Face-to-face with God, we will see clearly what we have believed by faith (see 1 Corinthians 13:12).

As long as we're alive, however, we should never cease our efforts to know, love, and serve God. We've discussed these three essential features of life in a linear fashion, but we practice them simultaneously. Remaining faithful every day to the work of knowing, loving, and serving God will pay off. We will grow closer to God in this life and be rewarded with the ultimate prize of eternal life with him in heaven.

It can be tricky to put all the steps we have discussed into practice. Don't give up. Persistence pays off. The obstacles will be there, but you can overcome them. Seek the help of the Holy Spirit, asking him especially to help you grow in the fruits of patience, faithfulness, and self-control. The Spirit will help you overcome any obstacle you encounter on your journey of faith.

Finally, I want you to know that God will reward your desire to know, love, and serve him. In fact, he has given you everything you need for your journey, because no matter how much you want to succeed, God wants you to succeed even more.

I'll pray for you. Please pray for me too.

Know and recall that there is no greater wealth and treasure, nothing more excellent and fruitful, than to love God and serve him, and that everything else passes like smoke and shadow.

—St. Charles Borromeo[7]

Notes

1. Charles de Foucauld, Prayer of Abandonment, EWTN, https://www.ewtn.com/catholicism/devotions/prayer-of-abandonment-361.

2. United States Conference of Catholic Bishops (USCCB), "The Corporal Works of Mercy," https://www.usccb.org/beliefs-and-teachings/how-we-teach/new-evangelization/jubilee-of-mercy/the-corporal-works-of-mercy.

3. Catholic Relief Services, "End World Hunger," https://www.crs.org/get-involved/learn/hunger.

4. The Divine Mercy, "Give Drink to the Thirsty," https://www.thedivinemercy.org/articles/give-drink-thirsty.

5. USCCB, "The Corporal Works of Mercy."

6. USCCB, "The Spiritual Works of Mercy," https://www.usccb.org/beliefs-and-teachings/how-we-teach/new-evangelization/jubilee-of-mercy/the-spiritual-works-of-mercy, quoting *United States Catholic Catechism for Adults*.

7. Ansgar Santogrossi, OSB, trans., *Charles Borromeo: Selected Orations, Homilies and Writings*, ed. John R. Cihak (New York, NY: Bloomsbury T & T Clark, 2017), 168.